Toxic Masculinity

Curing the Virus: Making Men, Smarter, Healthier, Safer

Stephen M Whitehead

First published in 2019
This revised edition
published in 2021 by
AG Books
www.agbooks.co.uk

ePub ISBN: 9781789821895
PDF ISBN: 9781789821901
This Paperback Edition: 9781789825251

For Gavin, Jay and Robert

Contents

Acknowledgements

So many individuals have been a positive part of my own masculinities journey that it would be impossible to list them all, though I acknowledge each of you now. Some of you are mentioned in the text, most are not. I owe every one of you a debt of gratitude.

As for this book, I am very grateful to the following for their comments, suggestions and for taking time to read early drafts and for their reviews of the book: Denry Machin, Sigrid Twibell, Roy Moodley, Carlton Rounds, Patrick Lee, Jing Yi Tan, Caroline Whitehead, Steve Cropper, and Gabriela Corbera. Thanks to Sheila French and Anissa Talahite for contributing to the original idea for a book on modern masculinity and the rise of women.

Finally, my thanks to Eva Pascal and Adam Dedman for the conversations we had over a decade ago during which for me at least, the concept of 'toxic masculinity' first got named and discussed.

Foreword

This book began its genesis many decades ago, long before I had any inclination to study, write, and question the gender norms which existed in my life from birth onwards. It has taken shape over seven decades, it is still taking shape though at some point one has to stop thinking, reflecting and start writing. Well, I have to.

I started writing *Toxic Masculinity* in the autumn of 2018 and the ebook version was subsequently published by AG in November 2019. This paperback version was published nearly 18 months later and for the most part is identical to the ebook version. In which case, you'll notice some important and relevant global events are not referred to or examined: the global covid-19 pandemic and the appalling responses to this crisis by many male politicians; the 2020 US Presidential election and the attempt to deny the democratic result; the George Floyd murder (USA); the global Black Lives Matter protests; the attack on the US Capitol by Trump supporters; the Sarah Everard murder (UK); the Boulder, Colorado shootings (USA); the first incel terrorist charge filed in Canada; and the rise in racist attacks and hate crimes against Asians, exemplified by the shootings in Atlanta, (USA) in March 2021.

That is one of the problems with toxic masculinity – it keeps on going, inflicting more pain. Every day, every week, every month, the deluge of male hate, violence, and anger continues more or less unabated.

At time of writing this Foreword, yet another example of Toxic Masculinity is surfacing and impacting global consciousness, especially in the UK. That is the overwhelming evidence of a 'rape culture' in UK schools, with many thousands of reports of sexual harassment, abuse and assault of female pupils posted on the www.everyonesinvited.uk website.

We seem to be living through an age of disillusionment and while that is sad maybe it is inevitable, if not essential. We have to let go of our myths and illusions and face reality if we are to mature as a global society and as individuals. Unfortunately, when it comes to confronting the toxic masculine culture at large in our schools, the illusion we have to let go of is the innocence of our children. The next generation of male rapists, murderers, abusers, torturers are in our schools right now. And they are already practicing for being toxic men.

- Do we recognise the problem?
- Are we happy with this situation?
- What are we going to do about it?

We cannot blame the children. We adults must take responsibility for the continuation or erasure of toxic masculinity in our lives, in our communities, in our world. No one is going to do this for us. We must act and do so now. This book is merely adding to the growing chorus for change as well as indicating where and how that change should come about if we are to progress the civilising process referred to in these pages.

But there is also evidence of progressive masculine values taking deeper root in society – not all men are a problem indeed a growing number are very much part of the solution and active in resisting toxic masculine values. And as for collapsed masculinity, introduced and examined in this book, even the Chinese government is now forced to recognise it as a distinct masculine identity. Though the Chinese government's somewhat predictable response is to see the emergence of more 'feminine Chinese males' as a big problem and one to be dealt with by 'developing more manly values in schools'. Will China's male leaders succeed in replacing collapsed masculinity with toxic masculinity in their young men? One would hope not, though from a sociological perspective it will be fascinating to see them try.

Stephen Whitehead
April 2021

Introduction

Teach men to be peaceful and the world will follow

I have been writing about men and masculinities for 30 years. This is my twelfth book. Each book has been part of an ongoing research not only into men but also the theories and dynamics of gender identity. Throughout these decades I have also been studying myself.

From the start of my journey into men and masculinities I realised that no man can or should venture into this field unless he has first declared himself to be a (pro)feminist. That is, he is fully aligned with the central tenets of feminism. Why? Because gender identity work is not apolitical. It is fundamentally about power. Gender is not now and never has been, neutral. And nor is sexuality. This is not a biological issue, it is a social one. Therefore, if you are a straight man and you wish to help change the traditional gender order, challenging and overturning hegemonic masculine values, attitudes, practices, then do so from a feminist standpoint. Any other standpoint means you are merely contributing to the problem.

At the same time, (pro)feminist men are not here to colonise feminism. We are here to strengthen it. And the best way to do so is to first recognise our relationship to that which we are investigating.

This is not me going off into some anxious hand-wringing guilt trip, it is simply me noting the truth of what I write about. Males are not born destined to be a problem. But many millions become a problem because of their sense of masculinity and how it manifests in actions and attitudes, not least towards women. No man can claim total innocence in this. We are all culpable to some degree.

But after three decades of research and writing, I can now see positive change on the horizon. This is signalled in the rising power of women and in the growing critique and discussion about men and masculinities. Imagine humankind to be a person taken to hospital with a long-term critical illness. The diagnosis must first identify and name the problem before it can set about treating it. That is where humankind is at right now. It has finally named the problem: toxic masculinity.

This stage of naming toxic masculinity engenders voices from all sides, of all genders and sexualities, to cry "foul" or "no more". There is a lot of 'calling out' and no doubt there is a lot more calling out to come. But this definitely needs to happen before we can get to the next stage in this process, which is to help males become healthier, smarter and safer.

It is, therefore, a noisy time to be writing about men. Which is in marked contrast to the deafening silence which surrounded the critical study of men back when I began my research, 30 years ago.

A benefit of ageing is that it allows one to acquire a widening perspective. I can recall the types of masculinity and femininity dominant in the UK in the 1950s, when I was a young boy. How times change. We thought the 1960s were the epicentre of a social revolution. Little did we realise, that decade merely signalled what was to come. If the sixties were about a male awakening, then the first two decades of the 21st century have seen a global female awakening. A sub-text throughout this book is this change in women; in their attitudes, expectations, confidence and sense of independence. And when we talk of independent women, what we really mean is women independent from men. This is without doubt the greatest social and political revolution ever to impact humankind. Humans have been around in some form or another for a very long time, but only now are we seeing the female of the species stand up and demand that men change. Only now are we seeing women, in every country, unite in opposition to male power, male violence, male aggression, masculinist assumptions of superiority. Alongside this are the millions of young women who do not assume the label 'feminist' but who nevertheless are making feminist decisions; e.g. choosing whether or not to get married, have children, get divorced, live a life as a single woman. A growing number of independent women are voting with their wombs: declining to bring children into the world. Women are finally tasting a little of the power which men have been feasting on for millennia.

I profoundly hope this movement does not slacken. Which is one reason why I've written this book. I feel an obligation to contribute. What you make of my contribution is for you to decide, though I had no choice but to write the book anyway. I started in November 2018 and six weeks later I'd written most of it – 60,000 words. It was all there inside me, waiting to come out. A three-decade accumulation of thoughts, research, knowledge, perspective. Backed up by seven decades living as a male, as a man. I admit that writing this book has been the most therapeutic experience of my career as a writer and academic.

As you read through the book you will encounter sections titled 'Reflections on a Journey'. This is me bringing myself into the narrative, adding a reflection or two. I could add a whole lot more but this book is not solely about me, it is about all men. It is written for all men.

Organisation of the Book

The book is structured into four parts and as a consequence it changes in tone over the chapters, so expect to read more theory, philosophy, sociology, political and analytical discussion in Part One and much less in the remainder of the book. This is necessary because some readers may have limited knowledge of the theories and research around men and masculinities, gender and identity. But having some background knowledge is necessary because any critical writer on gender and identity must first disabuse the reader of the 'gender as destiny' myth. That is, assumptions of biological determinism. There is nothing innate in men which is stopping them becoming smarter, healthier, safer.

Having provided the necessary context for understanding not only the changes taking place at this point in the human story, but also the contingency and multiplicity of male and female identities, the book then proceeds to Part Two, which describes the three dominant masculinities now apparent worldwide; toxic masculinity, progressive masculinity, and collapsed masculinity. I claim some small credit for helping bring TM (toxic masculinity) into the academic domain, but I was not one of those who pushed TM into the public space. As for 'progressive masculinity' and 'collapsed masculinity' these are my terms, though you may have come across them elsewhere. If so, I acknowledge those who got there before me. The final chapter of Part Two is where I test out these three dominant masculinities in respect of their relationship potential. Many women (and men) will definitely recognise male partners, significant others, friends, and perhaps even fathers, in the text. To aid understanding and discussion I have adopted a Q&A approach where appropriate.

Part Three is where I make a slight but necessary detour, firstly into women and TM, and secondly into TM and sexuality. There are probably books to be written on each of these two themes, though I aim only to introduce some important points. One point I seek to get across is that women cannot rely on men to bring about the changes needed. They must create their own resistance, with men such as myself in support. And there are a lot of men like myself in support, make no mistake. At the same time, to fail to recognise that many women do collude in TM is to ignore a key issue. Why they collude is one of the questions asked, and hopefully answered. This is not to say that I blame women for TM, far from it. It is recognising what I call 'the identity trick' at work here. As for sexuality, this is where the 'biology as destiny' theory unwittingly embraces the social contingency of gender identity. Some things we cannot change.

Finally, in Part Four, I get to the core of the question regards TM: *'How to bring about positive change in boys and men?'* What is involved in 'detoxifying men'? Not that much, in truth. It does not require pills, psychological testing, or even a reduction in the number of males. And locking men up certainly won't work. It simply requires a change in approach to raising boys and to helping men exit what I call the 'toxic masculine cave'. There are numerous examples of this happening right now around the world and in the most unexpected places. This is the good news. This is where we see men being proactive and embracing feminism, doing something really positive to help ensure the TM virus eventually gets controlled, if not eradicated.

So, the book ends on a positive note? Not quite. The final chapter spells it out; we are at a crossroads, facing four very different scenarios. While we seem to have arrived at this crossroads remarkably fast, in reality it has taken humankind millennia to get here. What you make of the four pathways and which direction you sense we are heading will determine your level of optimism for our future. Those who read early drafts of this book felt positive after reading. I hope you do too.

Part One

Gender Politics and Identity

Chapter One

Women Changing and Men Under Scrutiny

Women around the world are on the move, and a change is coming... a sense of empowerment has been unleashed and it will be very hard to stop it.

—French Journalist, Helene Daouphars

You cannot stop change. The younger generation know exactly what is out there. Everything's at our fingertips.

—First Saudi Arabian woman to climb Mount Everest, Raha Moharrak

I think what we want to say to the women of Indonesia is, don't be afraid of being different. Don't be afraid to shout your independence.

—Baceprot, all-female heavy metal band, Indonesian Muslims

I once said no thank you to a man when I was 19 and didn't have an excuse... and he punched me in the face. After that, whether or not I have a boyfriend, I say I do have. Being a woman is truly, constantly scary. It's like existing on thin ice.

—British actress, Jameela Jamil

A Global Awakening

In November 2018, *Oxford University Dictionaries* selected 'toxic' as the Word of the Year. This was exactly five years after the same university published my co-authored book, *'Gender and Identity'*, in which 'toxic masculinity' is briefly described, making myself and my co-authors arguably the first sociologists to enter this term into the academic lexicon. Go forward a few years and the term 'toxic masculinity' is ubiquitous. It has exploded into global consciousness, contributing to a new political awareness about male behaviour. Largely thanks to the MeToo movement and its offspring, there is now near 'open warfare' on that behaviour of men identifiable under the label 'toxic masculinity'. It is a devastating critique, a recognition that not only is "something is not quite right" with many males, but that a significant percentage of the global male population has acquired a form of masculinity which is misogynistic, self-destructive, deadly and damaging to all of us, even to the planet itself. This critical attention is no longer coming from only academics and activists, it is being referred to by musicians, film stars, politicians, artists, sportspeople; it is to be found on each continent, every city, most organisations, and is surfacing in a great many relationships.

Inspired largely by a revitalised global feminist awareness, in just a few years the topic of men and masculinities has gone from being 'invisible', of interest only to specialist academics like myself, to being of world-wide, mainstream concern. Media pieces on men and masculinity are surfacing globally and on a daily basis. In January, 2019, the American Psychological Association's (2018) 36-page report, detailing the dangers of 'traditional masculinity',[1] received worldwide attention. Reactions to the report ranged from the highly positive to the downright hostile, even causing a meltdown by host Piers Morgan on the UK breakfast television show, *Good Morning Britain* when he launched a furious rant over APA claims that traditional masculinity is toxic. This was closely followed by the Gillette razor advertisement which took aim at toxic masculinity, suggesting that 'men in 2019 could be doing better in some areas'. In May the same year, Gillette launched a second ad, this time highlighting fatherhood and trans male identity. There have been numerous television documentaries, including two by the BBC; one examining the MeToo movement in France ('*The French Resistance*'), the second, violent misogyny ('*Inside the Secret World of the Incels*'). UNESCO is now producing a *Handbook on Portrayals of Men and Masculinities in the Media* stating that 'concepts and norms of masculinity are inseparable from their representation in the media'.[2] Which is apposite because media outlets in most every country are now offering up daily discussions not just on toxic masculinity and male behaviour, but also on male psychology, a crisis of masculinity, toxic masculinity and the political environment, toxic masculinity and global warming, toxic masculinity and online trolling, and so on.

[1] APA (2018) *APA Guidelines for Psychological Practice with Boys and Men,* APA, August.

[2] UNESCO (2019) *Call for proposals to draft a handbook to sensitize and guide media professionals regarding the portrayal of men and masculinities in the media* (Section for Media Development and Society)

Yet despite this critical spotlight on men, there is no lessening of male abuse, male violence, patriarchal attitudes, and women's oppression. On the contrary, male violence and aggression towards women is nothing less than a pandemic, one which inevitably affects the life of every woman on the planet. While this is not a new situation, only now, after millennia of male aggression and violence, is human society starting to seriously question its inevitability and take active steps to stop it. And the first step in that direction is to identify and name the problem.

This book aims to contribute to the objective of eradicating toxic masculinity if not in current generations, then certainly in future ones. This is done not only by offering a critical examination of toxic masculinity, but by identifying two alternative global masculinities both of which offer smarter and certainly healthier ways of being a man: progressive masculinity and collapsed masculinity.

Embedded

As the book shows, toxic masculinity is not confined to the behaviours of a few aberrant males; it is embedded deep in the psyche of human society. So deep that for much of history we failed to recognise it. We simply saw male aggression, violence, rape and the general exploitation and marginalisation of women as part of some 'natural gender order'. It isn't. Through nothing less than the brutal application of physical force, men have declared themselves rulers since societies first formed and every time they ruled they made rules over women. In effect, down through history there has been a succession of powerful, often violent male leaders, most of whom legitimised patriarchy in their domain.

> If a superior man strikes a woman of superior class and thereby causes her to miscarry her fetus, he shall weigh and deliver ten shekels of silver for her fetus. If that woman should die, they shall kill his daughter.[3]

These are two of the 300 judgements devised by King Hammurabi, the ruler of the Babylonian Empire c1776 BC. A large part of Hammurabi's Code reads for what it is, probably the earliest human statement enshrining toxic masculinity in law, with women of whatever class identified as secondary citizens to men. Hammurabi devised his Code as a way to organise and control Babylonian society, with him at the apex. In reality, he was also defining the dominant codes of masculinity and femininity, and confidently assuming that men and women would follow them. Which they did. We are still living with the consequences of such a culturally devised gender binary. The difference today is that women are no longer blindly acceding to it.

---

[3]   Harari, Y. N. (2011) *Sapiens: A Brief History of Humankind.* New York: Vintage. (p.119)

As I discuss in the final chapter, this 'new sense of empowerment' that women around the world are experiencing and feeling, combined with the persistent ubiquity of toxic masculinity, takes human society to a crossroads. We've never been here before. Make no mistake, this is a first for humans. We cannot know what happens next, but for sure, in terms of gender power and identities, change is coming. This is not simply about competing 'identity politics' – it is about how human society wants to organise itself in the age of Artificial Intelligence (AI), super-advanced technology, a deteriorating environment, undermined democratic systems, and frightening social and economic inequalities. Toxic masculinity has prevailed throughout history. Are we going to allow it to prevail in the future? Indeed, can human society afford to allow it to prevail in the future? I think not. The stakes are not simply about male power and men's sense of identity; they are about the very survival of humankind.

There has to be a better way of organising ourselves. And that means no longer allowing individuals to rule by virtue of being male. The rising tide of female anger and resistance to toxic masculinity is, in my opinion, our only hope; the one bright light on an otherwise pretty grim horizon. But as I say, we are at the crossroads. In the final chapter I outline each of the four directions facing us, one of which society will definitely take.

The Questions

Having identified and named the problem of 'toxic masculinity', what next? What precisely is it? Where does it come from? Who has it? How does it work? How does one catch it? Can it be avoided? How does it interact with sexuality? What does it mean for women who encounter it? What does it mean for men who have it? How does it affect relationships? Is this the only masculinity out there? And, most importantly, can we get rid of it?

This book offers answers to all these questions. In so doing, it goes beyond toxic masculinity and into male identity work. It explores both the myths and the contemporary realities about men – and women. It raises difficult questions, not only for men but also for women; not least, how they may unwittingly collude in toxic masculinity as well as being the primary victims of it. To reiterate, toxic masculinity may be thriving but then it always has done; before 2013 it was known simply as 'traditional masculinity'. Fortunately, it is not the only masculinity now apparent in human society. And once we recognise and examine the other masculinities we instantly see that not all are problematic or lethal. Indeed, there are masculinities out there which are highly positive and to be encouraged. But how to encourage them? This book offers up some suggestions.

Human society has always evolved, constantly changed, but at this point in history it does feel that change is particularly rapid, especially profound and for many, quite disconcerting. But just where are we heading in terms of men, women and relationships? The answer to this question entirely depends on how successful we are in changing men, or at the very least, ensuring that future generations of males don't catch the TM virus. And we must make every effort to stop men catching this virus because not only is it killing others, it is killing them.

Recognising that we are all to some degree victims of TM, I welcome the fact that male behaviour is now coming under critical scrutiny. Before we can change men into ways of being which are healthier, smarter and safer, we need to have a conversation about them, and this book contributes to that conversation. At the same time, this focus is exposing the lack of understanding most people have in regard to gender identity and masculinities in particular. Few people fully understand masculinities nor how they come into being. They fail to recognise the different masculinities operating globally, and they are unsure as to how masculinity might be made more positive. This confusion then feeds into the resistance and insecurities which many men experience when their masculinity is put under the spotlight. It is hoped, therefore, that in reading this book you will gain insight into that most ubiquitous, misunderstood and yet most toxic characteristic of the human condition.

Chapter Two

Men, Masculinities, Identity

The Japanese word 'ohitorisama' will probably be unfamiliar to you, but almost certainly you'll have experienced it. It means, quite simply, 'being on your own'. In Japan, the singleton has become the predominant lifestyle to such an extent that 'ohitorisama' is the word used to describe this phenomenon: cinemas and restaurants now offer seating partitioned off for singles; bowling alleys and theme parks are adapting to a predominance of solo customers; even karaoke bars now provide young Japanese men and women with a *single* cubicle wherein they can belt out songs with gusto, with no one to argue over whether the next tune should be from The Eagles or Beyonce. This is the new 'super solo society' in action. A world where men and women interact at work and maybe on social media, but rarely, if ever, socially or, indeed, intimately.[4]

The ohitorisama lifestyle is evident in Japan's close neighbour, South Korea, where the popularity of the #No Marriage movement reflects the growing number of young women now rejecting marriage (and motherhood), leading the government to respond by offering incentives to encourage marriage and especially parenthood.[5] Head west to North America and the same phenomenon is apparent there; men and women increasingly living apart. The post-marriage society hit Quebec about ten years ago. Today, a majority of Canadians feel marriage is unnecessary.[6] Single people now make up the majority of the US population, up from just 22% in 1950.[7] The same trend is apparent across Europe, with Scandinavian countries as ever leading the way.[8] For the first time in its history, China is experiencing dramatic gender

[4]   https://www.japantimes.co.jp/news/2018/11/12/national/social-issues/going-solo-ohitorisama-japanese-art-alone

[5]   https://www.bloomberg.com/news/articles/2019-07-23/the-nomarriage-movement-is-adding-to-korea-s-economic-woes

[6]   http://angusreid.org/marriage-trends-canada

[7]   Klinenberg, E. (2012) *Going Solo.* New York: Penguin Books.

[8]   https://www.sociologylens.net/article-types/opinion/rise-single-households-european-union-impact-housing/18676

and familial changes leading not just to a falling birth rate and a rising divorce rate but to an increase in single women choosing to live as a single mother or choosing not to have babies.[9] Globally, single person households are becoming the most common living arrangement. Wherever one looks, the same pattern is apparent: single people living single lives broken only by increasingly brief periods of coupledom.

Anthropologist Nancy Smith-Hefner terms this 'waithood';[10] a state of forever waiting for the 'perfect life' before embarking on finding 'the one'. In reality, it is a world where if you are still single in your 30s, then you need not be worried; you are merely living the new normal.

However, what I see happening here is not just men and women living apart: I see men and women growing apart.

In this book I revisit this phenomenon because is it instructive. It tells us something very important about gender. And it tells us something very important about men, not least the myths that surround them. And debunking the myths surrounding men and masculinity is one of my aims.

One such myth is that masculinity and femininity are distinct but complimentary, naturally designed for the reinforcement, support and reproduction of the human species.

For tens of thousands of years, maybe since humans first walked out of Africa, most societies operated and developed around fairly strict sex roles; a public and private divide that even into the 1950s seemed entirely functional and natural to sociologists such as Talcott Parsons and Emile Durkheim, as well as to psychologists such as Freud and Jung. And then something changed. The contemporary philosopher Nassim Nicholas Taleb might describe it as a 'black swan'[11] moment, when an event occurred that was totally unforeseen but which changed everything, including our perceptions of reality.

For me, that 'black swan' moment was the publication in 1954 of 'The Second Sex' by Simone de Beauvoir.[12] It is rare that a single book or a single author changes the direction of history. But de Beauvoir arguably did. Her notion of women's (male-imposed) 'Otherness' resonated with women everywhere, and 65 years on it is still having an impact. If you are a feminist or in any way concerned with gender justice and equality, then *The Second Sex* is your foundational classic, one that contains many clues to the current problems confronting men.

[9] https://www.inkstonenews.com/society/instone-index-chinese-marriage-rate-hits-new-low/article/3004281

[10] https://marciainhorn.com/conferences/waithood-gender-education-global-delays-marriage

[11] Talelb, N.N. (2007) *The Black Swan: The Impact of the Highly Improbable.* London: Penguin

[12] de Beauvoir, S. (1953) *The Second Sex.* New York: Vintage

Of course, de Beauvoir's thesis was apposite through being aided by events, notably the rise of post-industrialisation during the post-war period, firstly in the West and ultimately globally. Why was this important? Because it began to erode not only the nuclear family, but also the concept of the male breadwinner. Nowadays, the male breadwinner nuclear family is almost an anachronism; something we remember existed not that long ago but which fewer families are experiencing today.

During the 1950s and into the 1960s, the space of just one generation, the emergence of modern feminist thinking aligned with dramatic social and economic changes to produce a perfect gender storm with far-reaching implications for both women and men. Consequently, by the late 1960s, some gender sociologists were starting to warn about an emergent 'male role identity crisis'[13] a notion that was for the most part dismissed. Very few people are dismissing this notion today.

If you study men in even the most cursory way, then you'll be aware that behind the male mask of apparent tolerance is often a seething anger, a hatred directed towards feminists and de facto towards women. It doesn't take a lot nowadays to trigger it. In fact, just being a woman with a voice, an opinion, can be enough to set the rage against 'all those feminazis' erupting. The irony is that these angry men focus on feminists and feminism, without of course understanding that it is as much history in the making which has destroyed their ingrained sense of masculine superiority, not simply the likes of feminists such as Greer, Butler, Dworkin, Daly, or indeed, de Beauvoir.

The Plastic, Testosterone Brain

The fear that lurks deep in the minds of many angry men today is, quite simply, extinction. Or at the least a disturbing sense that they have no purpose or role in society; they are surplus to requirements. From the rise of women to male educational underachievement; from MeToo to political correctness; from falling sperm counts to the decline of marriage; many men feel embattled. Some of these men have even given themselves a new identity – incel – meaning 'involuntary celibate', an ironic attempt at celebrating their singular condition. It is an existentialist fear which drives not only the most vehement misogynist, but also the casually sexist bloke. And they may have a point. As the radical feminist Mary Daly is attributed as indicating:

> If life is to survive on this planet, there must be a decontamination of the Earth. I think this will be accompanied by an evolutionary process that will result in a drastic reduction of the population of males.[14]

[13] For discussion see Whitehead, S.M. (2002) *Men and Masculinities: key themes and new directions.* (Chapter 2). Cambridge: Polity.

[14] https://en.wikipedia.org/wiki/Mary_Daly

But if this 'decontamination' of males does come about, it will not be because of men's inherent nature, it will be because they did not adapt to powerful social forces. And feminism is one such social force. It is not a unified movement. It is a way of thinking about oneself as a woman, and as a man, which challenges ideas of male superiority and seeks to overturn a gender order which stands on the backs of women. As this book explains regarding toxic masculinity, thoughts are like viruses.

One powerful anti-feminist virus is biological determinism; the idea that men's nature is fixed and determined from birth and to mess with it brings disaster.

To discuss gender identity with someone who believes in biological determinism is like trying to argue with a creationist that no, God didn't create the world 5000 years ago. In other words, it's impossible. The need that many people have to hold onto immutable ideas in the face of overwhelming evidence to the contrary is itself a study in human identity work. It doesn't matter whether or not a fact is true; the myth itself is all that counts. The reason is that the myth is invested in a person's ontological validation to the extent that to let go would, as sociologist Lois McNay puts it, "violate their sense of being".[15]

Genitalia does not determine identity. It does not determine how a person thinks. It does not determine what a person is capable of. Though sociologically, genitalia does have a lot to answer for.

The idea that our brains are gendered at birth and therefore all ensuing behaviour is naturally gendered is a false assumption. The brain is plastic: experience changes the brain and that interaction begins in the womb and carries on in our brains until death.

The danger with biological 'explanations' for human behaviour is that by being seen as 'natural' they are deemed to be irreversible. This is a convenient 'truth' too easily exploited by those with prejudiced agendas. The brain is not fixed, it is fluid; creating, reacting and adjusting to external stimuli. In other words, identity is work in progress, not an outcome.

There is little that is predictable, natural and inevitable about men. This is an important starting point for understanding them.

Next, we have the issue of sex hormones – testosterone and oestrogen – both of which are present to varying degrees in all humans, though it is testosterone that invariably gets wheeled out as the culprit for male violence and aggression, patriarchal cultures and the way in which society has evolved into a public/private dichotomy; men occupying positions of power and authority, with women, in some societies even today, confined to the home.

---

[15]   McNay, L. (2000) *Gender and Agency.* Cambridge: Polity. (p. 80)

But 'testosterone as male destiny' is another myth surrounding men. If you have a male child of primary school age and he is rumbustious, don't blame it on testosterone. Females the same age do not exhibit the same levels of disruptive behaviour even though they have very similar levels of testosterone as the boys. Nor do males experience a testosterone 'spurt' at any time of life.

In the UK, there are now a growing number of instances of very young boys, even kindergarten age, physically attacking teachers. This cannot be down to testosterone – these pre-puberty children do not have significant levels in their bodies anyway. Numerous studies show that male violence in societies and in schools can go up and it can go down, independent of unchanging levels of testosterone. Similarly, many studies show that aggressive behaviour may cause increases in testosterone, while nurturing behaviour can decrease testosterone in men – for example, in those men who are hands-on fathers.[16]

Trying to find a biological basis to male violence has understandably assumed something of a Holy Grail for many scientists around the world. If we could find the actual gene that causes men to become sexual harassers, rapists, murderers, rampant killers, torturers or bullies, then wouldn't that be great? We could erase or modify that gene with the result that life, indeed the whole world and humankind, would be so much better off. For some years now, scientists in China, USA, Japan and Europe have been trying to prove that variations in DNA were linked to men's violent behaviour. Indeed, so convinced were the Chinese scientists of the validity of this quest that they went a step further. More than ten years ago, armed with a load of government money, they went on a quest for the 'Warrior Gene'. These scientists didn't want to reduce the risk of male violence; they wanted to find ways of 'boosting aggression and building a better soldier'. However, ten years on and after studying blood samples from hundreds of youths convicted of violent crimes, they've come up with precisely – nothing. After spending millions of yuan and years of effort, the research was quietly declared a failure and stopped.

Researchers found that genes played an almost negligible role in young male's aggressive behaviour compared to environment factors such as poor social support, physical abuse and instability at home... A change of environment can lead to a change in human behaviour... The brain is plastic and life experience could significantly change the 'wiring' of neurons, affecting personality and behaviour.[17]

[16] http://healthland.time.com/2011/09/13/why-do-dads-have-lower-levels-of-testosterone/
      Fine, C. (2010) *Delusions of Gender: How our minds, society and neurosexism create difference.* New York: W.W. Norton; Hearn, J. (1998) *The Violences of Men.* London: Sage.

[17] https://www.scmp.com/news/china/society/article/2124661/china-calls-controversial-hunt-chinese-warrior-gene-children

With regards to males and their biology, the lesson is simply this: do not put men's behaviour, or their future, all down to hormones and genes. The world we grow up in, live in, and experience on a daily basis is much more influential and a more accurate predictor of our behaviour.

Male Identity

In August 2018, the American Psychological Association did something extraordinary. For the first time in its 127-year history it addressed issues arising from male identity work. It published a 36-page report designed to help psychologists specifically address the problem of traditional masculinity:

> Traditional masculinity ideology has been shown to limit male's psychological development, constrain their behaviour, result in gender role strain and gender role conflict and negatively influence mental health and physical health... [Masculinity ideology] is a particular constellation of standards that hold sway over large segments of the population, including: anti-femininity, achievement, eschewal of appearance of weakness, and adventure, risk and violence. [these behaviours link to] homophobia, bullying and sexual harassment.[18]

In effect, the APA is finally confirming what gender sociologists have long recognised, which is that traditional masculinity is a political ideology, not a biological state. This simple but profound statement by the APA throws the 'gender as biological destiny' myth out of the window. But one doesn't need a doctorate in psychology to understand why most men desire to be seen as masculine, even if they are not quite sure what masculinity actually is. Masculinity contains the codes of behaviour which they have internalised as essential for their validation as men. If you remove that masculinity, what are these men left with? Indeed, are they still men? For those men confused by the demands now being placed on them to become somehow less masculine, there is no easy answer. Few have the desire or the ability to make the transition from the dominant expression of masculinity they've invested their identities in, to what they perceive to be a subordinate one; especially if that subordinate masculine identity suggests, horror of horrors, femininity! Though, as I show in this book, alternative expressions of masculinity are gathering force around the world and all of them, in various ways, are closely associated with dominant expressions of femininity.

The path away from biological explanations for male behaviour takes us first to philosophy, and then on to sociology and psychoanalysis. What we learn on this journey is that to examine men we need to look not into their heads, but into their environment. Because it is within the social setting that masculinity gets named, normalised and validated.

---

[18]   APA (2018)

There is a compelling attraction to Rene Descartes' concept of circular self-validation. To claim "I think, therefore I am", solves a lot of existential problems. If I can doubt, question, perceive, and analyse, then surely 'I' must exist. Correct? Not quite.

Some two hundred years after Descartes passed away, a philosopher was born who was to render the 'I' pretty much redundant.

> I shall never tire of emphasising a small, terse fact, namely, that a thought comes when 'it' wishes, and not when 'I' wish.[19]

Frederick Nietzsche destroys the idea of a self-willing ego, claiming it to be at best an assumption and at worst a flight of vanity; the self in endless pursuit of its own recognition. Interestingly, one of the most durable of thinkers, Buddha, made the same point about the 'non-self' – only 2500 years earlier.

During the 1970s, another philosopher was to examine this question of identity in relation to sexuality and power and in the process became one of the most influential thinkers of the age. Michel Foucault's concept of the discursive subject reveals identity to be contingent, fluid and multiple, informed by the cultures, languages, behaviours and assumptions which surround us. In effect, the 'I' is a complex act of representation, rendered 'real' in the minds of the actor through partial and selective memory, narrative and habitual practice. It is through this identity work that the discursive subject emerges into society as the individual.[20]

Critiquing and deconstructing the notion of a sovereign self (individual) has been the aim of feminism since de Beauvoir, and arguably the most persuasive theories in this regard have come from contemporary theorist Judith Butler. Her concept of performativity draws heavily on Foucauldian theory and is described in her own words as follows:

> There is no gender identity behind the expressions of gender... identity is performatively constituted by the very 'expressions' that are said to be its results.[21]

It is in how we remember our selves, express our selves, and talk about our selves, that we engage in the process of rending the self into existence. This is the performative process described by Butler. We search for definition, for identification, simply because we must. We have no choice. Without an identity we have no independence, no sense of free will, no capacity for agency, no being and no belonging. But this process, real as it may appear in the moment, is amorphous. The psychoanalyst Jacques Lacan similarly stressed that there

---

[19] Nietzsche, F. (1997) *Beyond Good and Evil*. New York: Dover.

[20] Foucault, M. (1980) *Power/Knowledge*. New York: Pantheon Press.

[21] Butler, J. (1990) *Gender Trouble*. New York: Routledge, (p. 25)

was no individual beyond the representation, only the representation of the self that we claim to be us. In effect we are all in a quest for our selves, but that quest is not under our control. We cannot be defined 'nor can we escape all definition'.[22]

More recently, the philosopher Sam Harris put it like this:

You can do what you decide to do, but you cannot decide what you will decide to do.[23]

How does this relate to men and masculinities? Well, it tells us that men do not consciously decide to exhibit a particular form of masculinity; it is invariably infused in their minds through cultural osmosis, a process that certainly starts from birth and continues in unpredictable ways all their lives. In short, masculinity is neither inevitable nor stable. Which makes it both very insecure and highly vulnerable.

It is necessary to see masculinity not as a biological product of maleness, but as the way in which society has, over time, identified certain types of behaviour with males and the opposite types of behaviour with females. This artificial gender binary is at the very least a political division because it has suited (straight) men much more so than it has suited anyone else; e.g. women and LGBT+ people.

Masculinities are those behaviours, languages and practices, existing in specific cultural and organizational locations, which are commonly associate with males and thus culturally defined as not feminine.[24]

Just because society makes an assumptive leap between genitalia and behaviour does not mean it exists as a natural and inevitable consequence. So why do we continue to make this leap? Because it appears less complicated, slots humanity into labels, creates a gendered binary which we feel compelled to relate to, and reinforces the gender stereotypes that have been handed down to us through history. Plus, it suits some to continue to make this leap because they have invested not only their selves in it, but also their futures.

In short, humanity has fallen for a one of the biggest linguistic deceptions in history – the gendering of behaviour to produce an artificial but highly politicised code whose fundamental effect, if not aim, is to differentiate between male and female, with men the historical beneficiaries through the creation of a patriarchal dividend – whether they seek it or not.

And if it weren't for a few 'Black Swans', maybe this deception would have gone on unnoticed for millions of people. Well, not anymore. We now

[22]   Sarup, M. (1993) *Poststructuralism and Postmodernism*. London: Harvester Wheatsheaf.

[23]   Harris, S. (2012) *Free Will*. New York: Free Press.

[24]   Whitehead, S. M. and Barrett, F.J. (eds) *The Masculinities Reader*. Cambridge: Polity (p.15)

recognise that this historical gendering need not inevitably apply to the present and certainly not to the future. Humanity is now fully aware of diversity. Globalisation and technology have exposed the fallacy of the gender binary, as well as the fallacies surrounding sexual, racial and ethnic stereotypes. We live in a rich and varied social soup, not in 'comfortable' human social compartments, with straight white men naturally positioned at the top of a social hierarchy and the rest located beneath them.

The most powerful indicator of our identity is upbringing. None of us chooses when and where we are born, but it is this simple fact that hugely influences what sort of person, man or woman, we might become. *You may be a flaming liberal in New York, but it's likely you'd be a flaming conservative if you grew up in Wyoming.*[25]

Identity work is a mix of association and disassociation. It is what I am not that defines, in my mind, what I am. We hang on to these codes of behaviour, these ever-present ideologies in the hope of existential purchase. Foucault calls them 'dominant discourses'. So, the 'flaming liberal' in New York is this person because they have been surrounded from birth by a range of dominant discourses many of which are not only different to those surrounding the 'flaming conservative' in Wyoming but are totally alien to them.

But the liberal and the conservative have one thing in common; they will grasp onto their respective identities with as much determination as the person hanging onto a sheer rockface. Out of fear. Fear of losing their selves. Fear of plunging into the existential abyss.

To understand how masculinity works and why it is so precious to many men it is necessary, therefore, to first recognise that none of us is fixed in our identity. We are forever adapting, changing, creating, while being shaped by forces we cannot wholly recognise, never mind control. At the same time, we each have a deep and profound existential desire to be and become. We fear 'not being' more than we fear death itself. We exist as a life force which demands identification, validation, recognition and acceptance if it is to acquire not only meaning, but very likely contentment and happiness. If males grow up in a culture which has defined masculinity in a very narrow way, then we cannot be shocked and surprised if those males gravitate towards that narrow definition. And in turn replicate it as adult men. Why would they not?

Until recently, critically scrutinising masculinity was not something that absorbed many people. When I wrote my PhD thesis on men and masculinities in the early 1990s, I was one of just a handful of global academics researching this area. But questioning their masculinity is a phenomenon that men are now having to grapple with, and not just in the West, which can be challenging

---

[25]   David Brooks, quoted in Whitehead, Talahite and Moodley (2013) *Gender and Identity: key themes and new directions.* Don Mills, Ontario: Oxford University Press (p. 293)

because what they assumed was natural and constant turns out to be neither. What they assumed to be prized turns out to be problematic. What they are, is not what the 21st century apparently needs nor wants. Which leaves them where?

The Harvey Weinstein exposure, leading directly to the MeToo Movement, was another perfect 'Black Swan' moment, one that changed everything. That same moment is now demanding that men reflect, adapt. But can they? Are they prepared for such a change? And what are we expecting that they change into? These questions merely emphasise how important it is that we understand (toxic) masculinity and recognise the forces which drive it, validate it and render it highly problematic both for men and for women. And one of the most potent but corrosive aspects of toxic masculinity is its relationship to power.

Men and Power

The umbilical-like association of men to power cannot be overstated, nor should it be underestimated. If maleness speaks of anything, it speaks of power. Just ask a typical primary school age boy whether he thinks he is stronger and better at sport than the girls in his class and I guarantee the answer will be "yes, of course". The fact that he is wrong doesn't even cross his mind. But he is. In all measures of physical performance, there is no statistical difference between the capabilities of girls and boys until they reach high-school age.[26] But through subconsciously learning that boys should be stronger than girls, the gender binary gets reinforced, affecting the behaviours and attitudes of children even before they reach kindergarten. By the time most boys reach primary school, they already imagine themselves superior to girls.

The equation that physical strength and performance equals power is highly persuasive and readily feeds into the masculine subconscious, thereby creating a compelling template from which men can bolster their sense of maleness. But not every man is a world-class boxer or Premier League footballer. So how do men without recourse to heightened physicality nourish their 'maleness = power' association?

For much of the 20th century, there was one area which remained immune from the intrusions of the female, and that was leadership. Whatever the professional realm, whether it be politics, business, law, finance, uniformed services, civil service, science, health, engineering, technology or education, men dominated at the top. And for the most part this remains the case, though the barriers are slowly crumbling with women leaders now emerging in every field from Generals to Prime Ministers, Corporate CEOs to Quantum

[26]   https://n.neurology.org/content/88/16/1512   https://www.smh.com.au/lifestyle/when-it-comes-to-sport-boys-play-like-a-girl-20170804-gxp2gq.html

Researchers, Astronauts to Bankers. Importantly, women are increasingly seen as the gender best suited to leadership:

> *I think women do leadership particularly well because they take people with them. They often cut through all the nonsense and see 'what are the priorities here, what are the important things to come out of the decision I've got to make?'. I think they bring a total lack of testosterone to the decisions that have to be made...The gender balance in the {British} military will gradually improve over the next 10 years. And that isn't going to be a benevolent action, it's going to be by necessity, because the complexities that we have in defence are going to mean the big chap mastering commander skills we think of as leadership are just going to fall away. We'll need people who can really manage complex programmes and projects and that's absolutely gender neutral.*[27]

Globally, there has been a rapid and profound shift in attitudes towards macho leadership, leaving men who are unable to change, out on a limb.

> *We live in a world that's increasingly social, interdependent and transparent. And in this world feminine value are ascendant. A recent global survey of 64,000 people across 13 countries shows that traditionally feminine leadership and values are now more popular than the macho paradigm of the past.*[28]

This trend is apparent now in an increasing number of international corporations, not least Alibaba.

> *52% of our company is women. 35% of our management staff is women. 23% of our senior management is women. We've had a female CEO, a female chairman, a female CPO, CFO, etc. Our company also has a lot of female engineers, and of course a lot of female PhDs... Women are going to be very powerful in the 21st century. Because last century people cared about muscle. This century people will care about wisdom.*[29]

At time of writing, the leaders of both the London Fire Brigade and the London Metropolitan Police are women. An historic first for London and the UK.

> *[Our appointments] show that things are changing. We're both the first of our kind, and I think it's just opened the door to show that things will be different in the future. As women, we can do the job differently... and without any sense of force authority... The macho image has to go... the issue for some of the male firefighters is that if a woman can do the job then it's not the big hero job is*

[27] John Louth quoted in https://www.independent.co.uk/news/uk/home-news/militarys-brass-ceiling-to-melt-as-women-take-command-10093608.html

[28] http://www.johngerzema.com/books/athena-doctrine   https://www.thoughtco.com/qualities-of-women-leaders-3533957

[29] https://www.scmp.com/video/2099485/hire-many-women-possible-jack-mas-secret-alibabas-success

was. It de-machos their role. Which is fine. We have to change the perception of a six-foot muscled bloke who can kick a door down.[30]

If anyone had any doubts left that the most effective form of leadership is not macho posturing and exhibiting threatening behaviour, then look no further than New Zealand PM Jacinda Ardern. Following the horrific killing of 50 people at two mosques in central Christchurch in March 2019, 38-year-old Ardern demonstrated to the world maturity, sincerity, emotion, strength, compassion and, most importantly, empathy. In so doing, she helped unify a mourning nation.

> *She is like the mother of the nation. When it comes to events like this, here touch is near perfect. The way Trump and others talk, tough talk after terror attacks, all that is posturing. And sometimes it is designed to mask weakness, sometimes it is a thirst for revenge. Ardern is doing none of that. It is a leadership style that particularly suits New Zealand. New Zealand does have a dark side, it does have racism. But what she is doing is giving us a moment to confront these demons, this darkness, and change our ways.*[31]

From politics to business, smart thinking now accepts that 'feminine traits' must be apparent in leaders and managers before they are appointed. Which is bad news for a great many men. Because for every woman appointed to a leadership role, whether it be Prime Minister, Police Chief, or CEO, that job is no longer going to a guy. This is the reason why gender equality is a zero-sum power game, as well as being something of an oxymoron: a contradiction in possibilities, not a feasible material reality. In other words, for women to acquire power, men will have to relinquish it.

Why? Because the power that men have historically wielded has been power over women. Once they are denied that gender power, then they no longer have power as a gender.

There is even a word for it: emasculation.

Interestingly, there is no equivalent word for women and femininity.

What is revealed here is the fact that all power is inherently unstable, especially the power that comes from being born male. Despite patriarchy being the norm in most societies for millennia, it can still be undermined. It is being undermined. All it requires is a change of thinking, a change of language, a reassessment of what is 'normal'.

Power circulates; it is never secure; it sticks in some places and not in others, and that is especially so in organisations. For example, if you wish to examine

[30] https://www.theguardian.com/uk-news/2017/mar/05/dany-cotton-london-fire-brigade-commissioner-interview

[31] https://www.theguardian.com/business/grogonomics/2019/mar/23/jacinda-envy-why-the-days-of-a-middle-aged-white-male-leader-could-be-over

where power is located in any organisation, don't just interview the leader. You need to go through the system. The notion that power is only and ever hierarchical is to misunderstand the nature of power. A culture, a sub-culture, can be masculine in orientation even if the leader is a woman. The gender theorist Arthur Britton devised the term 'masculinism' to explain this:

> *Masculinism is the ideology that justifies and naturalises male domination, as such it is the ideology of patriarchy. Masculinism takes it for granted that there is a fundamental difference between men and women, it assumes heterosexuality is normal, it accepts without question the sexual division of labour, and it sanctions the political and dominant role of men in the public and private spheres.*[32]

Any setting where traditional gender values prevail, where men dominate over women, where homophobia exists, or where it is assumed that women are weaker than men, be it a nation state, community, organisation, a family, or just a work team, then that setting is masculinist. And the power that emits from that environment draws validation from a gendered ideology. Indeed, men can only 'justify' this domination by recourse to such thinking. Once they are confronted with the fact that women are equally capable, if not better than men in many areas, then not only is their power undermined, so is their masculine identity. They are, indeed, 'de-macho'd'.

Those men who have invested their sense of masculine self in the ideology of masculinism face some testing times. They can no longer readily embrace this ideology without appearing dysfunctional as males, without seeming out of touch with the zeitgeist. Unless, of course, they retreat or ensure they are surrounded only by likeminded men who act as corroborators in their resistance against "modern women". This dilemma was developing for men long before the MeToo movement kicked off; that merely catapulted the issue into the media spotlight and gave millions of women an opportunity to voice long-felt frustrations and anger.

Of course, adult men still have one 'natural' advantage over most females, and that is physical strength. For many, any desire they may have to retain some semblance of traditional gender power will manifest itself as violence. In Chapter 6, I explain what it means if a man is a 'resister', increasingly denied the opportunity to exert traditional masculinity through the family, work, organisations, or even on the sports field.

With male violence against women being a pandemic, with 'up to 70% of women having experienced physical and/or sexual violence from a man'[33] then

---

[32] Brittan. A. (1984) *Masculinity and Power*. Oxford: Basil Blackwell (p.4)

[33] http://www.unwomen.org/en/what-we-do/ending-violence-against-women/facts-and-figures

the claim by radical feminist Andrea Dworkin that all men are potential rapists rings as true as ever.

Every woman's son is her potential betrayer and also the inevitable rapist or exploiter of another woman.[34]

Of all the radical feminists, the late Andrea Dworkin nailed it. And in so doing she made us all confront a horrible truth. As unpleasant as it is for any man, myself included, to read her unfettered analysis of men and their abuse of women, the global evidence overwhelming shows it to be a fair and accurate reflection of reality. This raises the question: are all men the same?

Multiple Masculinities

Simon is 30, single, and a professional poker player. He lives in Atlanta, USA. He works out at the gym at least five times a week, has the body to prove it, and is a virgin. Simon has never even kissed a woman, well, other than his mother. He has never dated a woman and has no interest in dating men. He is not asexual, he is simply sexually inhibited.

Marcel is 45, married, and a lawyer. He lives in Paris. This is his second marriage, and he has four children from the two relationships. Marcel has a lover, his secretary. His wife knows but Marcel doesn't know she knows. His wife also has a lover, her best friend's brother. Neither Marcel nor his wife are sexually inhibited, but they are living a convenient lie.

Ali is 50, married, and owns a school servicing company in Penang, Malaysia. He got married at the age of 23, has two children, and has only ever had sex with one woman – his wife. He has, however, had sex with lots of men. As a Muslim man, living in Malaysia, this is risky. So, every month, Ali drives north to the Thai border, crosses over and takes the road to Yala, the city where he can play freely.

Three men, three different types of masculinity, three different sexualities. One of these men is a feminist, believes in women's rights and in equal opportunities. Another man is educated, articulate, and has fascist inclinations. The third man is living out a confused existence, torn between his nature and his culture.

You can probably work out which is which. Yes, they are in the order I present them. These men exist. You'll likely know men who are very similar. They are each trying to deal with conflicting desires, unachieved expectations and externally imposed cultural prohibitions. They are all male by virtue of having a penis. But how they live with their penis, and their emotions, is rather different. Only one of them is angry at women and to an outsider he would appear to have the least reason to be. All of them are fearful of something and that something resides deep inside themselves, not in society. It is how they individually deal with that fear which reveals the sort of man they are.

[34]   Dworkin, A. (1981) *Our Blood*. New York: Tarcher Perigee

The very term 'masculinity' is problematic, not least because by saying it we reinforce not only the gender binary (if there is a masculinity then there must be a femininity) but moreover, the notion of male singularity. We use language and words to give meaning to an otherwise incomprehensible world. It is how we try and make sense of the nonsensical and of our selves. But words are also weapons and get used as such.

However, men are not all the same: they don't all have the same behaviours, they don't all think the same and they definitely don't all have the same masculinity. Masculinity is multiple. Within every male it will correspond, sometimes problematically, with a host of other identity variables which, taken together, serve to constitute an individual 'man', at least on the surface. In feminist studies, this dynamic is known as 'intersectionality':

> *Every individual exists at the intersections of many aspects of self and social powers... race, sex, sexuality, ability, ethnicity, age, culture and class [all act to] "produce" the individual... None of us is simply man or woman: we have a race, an ethnicity, a nationality, a sexuality, plus many other facets to our being. Each facet, importantly, has some influence on the other.*[35]

But to simply say that masculinity is multiple and all men are different isn't the whole story, because there are patterns and from these patterns there emerge dominant types of masculinity.

When I was growing up in the north of England in the 1950s the dominant type of masculinity was white, heterosexual, working class, uneducated and traditional. Men doffed their caps at women; they left school at 15 to work in factories or go into the armed forces; they were married by 21 and became fathers shortly afterwards; they drank beer in pubs and smoked Woodbines; they read the *Daily Express*; they went to football matches on a Saturday afternoon; they had day trips to Morecambe, and when they got home at night their dinner was waiting on the kitchen table.

That has all disappeared. As have the men, though their masculinity lingers, like the smoke from the Woodbine cigarette.

But it is just smoke; a memory, nostalgia, a mirage. And because it no longer exists as a dominant way of being a man, many men seek to reconstruct it. In the UK, you can see it being reconstructed by English men flying the Flag of St George. You'll hear it being reconstructed at football matches when England is playing. And you'll read about one of the consequences of that reconstruction when a female celebrity or politician reveals the level of misogynism directed towards her by male online trolls.

---

[35] Whitehead, S.M., Talahite, A., Moodley, R. (2013) *Gender and Identity*. Don Mills, Ontario: Oxford University Press (p.72)

You can see and hear the same yearning for a return to 'traditional masculinity' in many places, not only the UK. These men have much in common: they are not happy with multiculturalism, women's rights, feminism, and the 'decline of man'. They may not live a traditional masculinity but by heck they want it back – or a version of it. They can almost smell the Woodbine in the breeze. This is enough to drive them to gravitate towards it with the same impulse that causes Ali to gravitate towards Yala once a month – because it makes them feel good and it serves to satisfy their need to be a 'real man'. The irony is, of course, that the extinct masculine identity these men yearn to make real has, by their very actions, become corrupted in the present.

But what is a 'real man'? No one can tell you, and certainly not these men. Because a real man only exists in his imagination. The three individuals briefly described above are all real men, but which you consider to be the most 'manly' is for you to decide. Personally, it is not a question I ever ask of men, nor of myself, the reason being that the pursuit of manliness is pointless: manliness is a chimera. You can chase it as hard as you like, but if you have to chase it at all then self-evidently you don't have it.

Which brings me, finally, back to 'ohitorisama'. If you look at photos of Japanese men from the 20th century you'll see two types dominate: the military man and the salaryman. The former defined Japanese masculinity certainly until 1945. Thereafter, it started to decline. It was quickly replaced by the latter; the salaryman masculinity which corresponded with Japan's emergence as a post-war world leader in business, engineering, technology and manufacturing.

Although these male types appeared different, they were identical in several respects. They were dutiful, loyal, respectful to authority and willing to subdue their individuality to the needs of the organisation and therefore to Japanese society. In other words, Japanese men merely swapped the armed forces for Toyota. They gave their lives to each system and were expected to do so. Women stayed at home and enabled this dedication to Japanese society to be total, with strict gender roles as the glue that kept it together.

Communality and traditional gender roles still hold sway over Japanese society to this day, but it is rapidly changing. In a few decades Japanese masculinity has become more feminised, and in some regards, quite explicitly so. This process has seen the emergence of a softer masculinity; the 'Herbivore Males' (see Chapter 5).

Today, if you ask Japanese Millennial males how they feel about themselves as men and how they feel about women, then you'll likely get answers such as these.[36]

[36]   https://www.theguardian.com/world/2013/oct/20/young-people-japan-stopped-having-sex   https://www.reuters.com/article/us-japan-herbivores/japans-herbivore-men-shun-corporate-life-sex-idUSTRE56Q0C220090727

Since I was a child, I hated people telling me, 'Behave like a man'… I don't think my parents' way of life is for me. I still struggle between the traditional notion of how men should be and how I am… I've no interest in pursuing women. (Roshinante, 31)

I've had lots of female friends that I am attracted to, but you weigh up the risk and benefits and come to the conclusion that things are best left as they are. (Moto, 30)

I don't have a girlfriend and never have. I am a virgin and I guess that is how I will remain. I could get married in the future, but it is not that important. I enjoy my life as it is. (Akinari, 40)

I am not interested in following the lifestyle of my parents. I don't date women and have never had sex. I enjoy anime, karaoke, and manga, but most of my social life is spent on my own. I don't see a problem with that. (Maki, 28)

What has been emerging with Japanese males over the past decade or more is now spreading to other countries in Asia: South Korea, China and Hong Kong. This is no longer a localised masculinity; a unique and strange by-product of Japanese culture. It's becoming regionalised, widespread, and could well emerge globally in the near future. Indeed, there are signs of it already doing so.

As I say, masculinity is a virus; one that takes root first in our imagination then spreads to our behaviours, at which point it gets exposed in our relationships to women and other men. And every time we act it out, we are encouraging it to spread.

Part Two

The Three Global Masculinities

Chapter Three

Toxic Masculinity

Anyone writing about toxic masculinity is assured of one thing – there is no shortage of examples. During the 48 hours that I began work on this chapter, these were just a few of the international news headlines relating to toxic masculine behaviour:

Saudis 'tortured female activists by electrocution and flogging'

Teen girl auction on Facebook without company's bosses noticing

Gunman kills three people at Chicago hospital

Man deliberately mowed down Chinese children, killing 5

Payout over British primary schoolboys' sex assaults on girl, 6

"Why I send photos of my genitals to women"

One dead and eleven wounded in attack at Chinese college

Six boys arrested for 'gang sex attack' at Toronto private school

Allegations of rape and child molestation made against British youth charity volunteers

Man hurled racist slurs and punch at FedEx driver then died after he was punched back.

Outrage in Paraguay after Brazil cartel boss kills woman in his prison cell

South Korean cult leader gets 15 years in jail for raping followers

Quadruple stabbing in north London linked to minicab shooting

Girl who wrote essay on gun violence is killed by stray bullet

26-year-old man charged in 'biggest sexual offence charge' in Norway's history

Mobs attack women near India Hindu temple

On the first day of that week, Monday 19th November 2018, The Gun Violence Archive of America recorded 63 separate shootings, leaving at least 11 dead.

Horrific as that violence is, it was nothing remarkable – just another seven days during which men murdered, raped, abused, violated and exercised their power over women. But its true horror is revealed by its sheer ordinariness: male violence and aggression so common that society has become hardened to it.

Femicide is the world's unseen crisis. But nurse Dawn Wilcox is one woman keeping count. From her home in Texas, she runs Women Count USA, and every day she adds 50 more names of women killed by men in America. As Dawn puts it:

> Violence against women is so ubiquitous that it is invisible. That one nurse in Texas can find 1,600 women that have been allegedly murdered by men in the United States in a single year, that is staggering... Violence against women is normalized. And because it's normalized we don't see it as a crisis.[37]

One reason why we don't confront the horror of male violence against women is that too often we'd prefer to assuage our complicity and blame the victims instead: 'wrong place, wrong time', 'shouldn't have been wearing a short skirt', shouldn't have gone home alone in that taxi', 'shouldn't have stayed out late', 'should have checked the lock on that window', 'shouldn't have married him', should have not been there at all. Just unlucky. How many women have been unlucky? How many more will be unlucky?

Toxic masculinity is without doubt the most damaging and dangerous form of masculinity out there. It is damaging and dangerous not only for society but also for the men who have it. Unfortunately, it is also the most common. It encompasses everything from ritualised hazing in universities, to the macho politics and posturing of men such as Duterte, Trump, Putin, Erdogan and Bolsonaro. It is explicit in video games, many sports, most brotherhoods and all criminal gangs. The armed forces of every country actively encourage it. It is embedded in the machismo of Central and South American cultures, the tribalism of Africa, the religious hegemonies of the Middle East and the caste systems of South Asia. The toxic masculine virus has infected every region on earth – nowhere has proved immune. Children are expressing it at pre-school, bosses are expressing it at work, the internet is expressing it everywhere.

Are Things Getting Worse?

In which case, can one conclude that as far as global gender politics is concerned, things have never been worse?

[37] https://www.theguardian.com/us-news/2019/apr/11/the-nurse-tracking-americas-epidemic-of-murdered-women

Actually, things have definitely been worse. At least according to psychologist, Steven Pinker:

> It's not just violence that one sees progress, but in poverty, in illiteracy, in access to small luxuries like beer or televisions. The percentage of the world getting an education, in gender parity in education – girls are going to school all over the world. Even in Afghanistan and Pakistan, the world's most retrograde countries, the rate of female education has increased.[38]

Yes, counter-intuitively, the evidence does reveal an unmistakable trend towards less violence, more freedom of expression, higher levels of education, greater gender equality and more individual empowerment. And that is not just in the West but globally. Much as it may surprise you to learn, evidence does suggest that, globally, humankind is slowly going through the 'civilising process' suggested by the German sociologist Norbert Elias many decades ago.[39]

However, it is no coincidence that any 'civilising process' as predicted by Elias and now empirically confirmed by Pinker, has occurred in tandem with the emergence of modern feminism. All the points made by Pinker refer to changes in the behaviour of women and a change for the better in terms of their rising expectations and aspirations. *This change has fed directly into the emergence of smarter, healthier forms of masculinity emerging globally over the past few decades.* For me, that is the single biggest factor in any rise in civilising behaviour. For feminism was never only about women, and is not now. The rise in feminism has been increasingly impacting on men at least since the 1970s and that impact is now going mainstream. Increasing numbers of men are waking up to the fact that feminism is liberating for them also, not just for women. We cannot get more civilised by behaving as we've done throughout history. There has to be an intervention and feminism has been that intervention. The rise in women's expectations is percolating through to all the genders and all the sexes.

But while our expectations are now higher than in the past, it needs to be recognised that we are starting from a depressingly low base line. During my childhood, gay men were imprisoned, single mothers risked being put in mental health institutions and having their babies taken away, orphaned children were shipped off to Australia in their thousands, landlords were allowed to put up 'no blacks allowed' signs, few people had ever heard the term 'paedophile', equal opportunities legislation was not even an aspiration, only 1.2% of women went to university, and the patriarchal family was the norm for all social classes.

And that was the UK during the 1950s and into the 1960s. Go back to the first half of the last century, which saw countless millions slaughtered in the name

[38]   https://www.nytimes.com/2018/11/19/science/steven-pinker-future-science.html

[39]   Elias, N. (1969) *The Civilizing Process*. London: Blackwell.

of empire, fascism, communism, religion or simply because they happened to be in the wrong place at the wrong time, and one can see very clearly that life was pretty frightful for most people. And this violence was led by men, executed by men, done in the name of man, and carried with it the expectation of being manly.

It is not too difficult for an educated 21st century man or woman to spot the gender in the word 'history', but throughout history few people have identified war and violence as a particular problem of men. I am not aware of anyone back in the 1930s accusing Stalin, Hitler or Mussolini of having toxic masculinity. Which tells us that perspective is everything, as is hindsight.

Men have been performing toxic masculinity for as long as there have been men. And for the most part this form of masculinity has gone unchallenged – it has rarely been analysed as problematic male behaviour. Humanity assumed this was how men behaved; it was in their nature. Much of humanity still believes this myth. Masculinity didn't suddenly become toxic with the introduction of the MeToo movement. *The dominant form of masculinity has always been toxic.* The difference today is that many women and increasing numbers of men are not accepting this as the 'norm' for males. They are, quite rightly, challenging this gendered condition and expecting something better from men.

In other words, masculinity only became recognised as being 'toxic' when society labelled it so. And since 2016, society has done just that.

However, labelling 'toxic' that which has historically been accepted as 'traditional male behaviour' creates some problems. There are now a lot of very confused, fearful and angry men left stranded with a masculinity which once was valued, once was the norm, once was aspirational, but which is now recognised for what it is: damaging and corrosive.

The Definition

Societal change can be overwhelming, especially in the age of social media, but it is neither neutral nor benign. It operates through so many unforeseen variables that predicting the future is impossible.

Who could have predicted the term 'toxic masculinity' becoming so ubiquitous that *Oxford University Dictionaries* would make 'toxic' the 2018 Word of the Year? Certainly not I. When I and my fellow authors introduced the term into the academic lexicon in 2013 we certainly recognised its potency, though perhaps not its potential.

Within many masculine cultures and value systems, male aggression is not considered problematic; indeed, it is actually lauded. Criminal gangs, the armed forces, militaristic and totalitarian societies are where we are most likely to witness and experience "toxic masculinity": that is, aggressive male behaviour that is fundamentally corrosive to society and to individuals, including those who perform it: such behaviour continues to be expressed by, indeed attracts to it, males of all ages, cultures, ethnicities and social statuses.[40]

The key word in that quotation is 'aggressive'. Toxic masculinity is nothing if not aggressive in essence, and as I discuss below, that aggression can be both externalised and internalised by the person performing it.

But many years before the publication of that definition, gender sociologists like myself had already recognised dominant masculinity as a major problem affecting global society. And the name we gave that problem was 'hegemonic masculinity'.

Hegemonic Masculinity

Hegemony refers to the ability to impose a particular culture, value system or social system on a group, organisation or society. The word originates from Antonio Gramsci and is used especially by Marxist and structuralist theoreticians. The term 'hegemonic masculinity' was first devised by Carrigan et al[41] but is mostly associated with gender sociologist Raewyn Connell.[42]

Hegemonic masculinity [is] a form of male behaviour and expression of male identity that seeks to reinforce men's power and patriarchal values. Based on characteristics such as competition, ambition, self-reliance, physical strength, aggression, and homophobia.[43]

The image of masculinity that is perpetrated [by hegemonic masculinity] involves physical toughness, the endurance of hardships, aggressiveness, a rugged heterosexuality, and unemotional logic...[44]

Toxic masculinity is, in effect, the mainstream term for hegemonic masculinity, with the latter being the concept adopted by sociologists and psychoanalysts since the late 1980s.

For over thirty years, as a theory of male power, hegemonic masculinity has been used extensively by gender theorists to examine male behaviour in countless social and organisational settings. And in that regard it has proved

[40]   Whitehead, S.M., Talahite, A., Moodley, R. (2013) *Gender and Identity.* Don Mills, Ontario: Oxford University Press (p.246)

[41]   Carrigan, T., Connell, B. and Lee, J. (1985) 'Toward a New Sociology of Masculinity', *Theory and Society,* 14, pp.551-604.

[42]   Connell, R. W. (1995) *Masculinities.* Cambridge: Polity.

[43]   *Gender and Identity* (201 (p.22)

[44]   Barrett, F.J. (2001) *Hegemonic Masculinity: The US Navy* in Whitehead and Barrett (eds) *The Masculinities Reader,* Cambridg: Polity. (p.81)

very useful. However, as an explanation of male identity the term has also been subject to critique, not least because we must not assume a simple or linear relationship between how men act, how men perceive themselves, how men want to behave, and the naked pursuit of male power exemplified in the term hegemonic masculinity.

It is clear that not all men perform hegemonic masculinity, nor seek to. Many men actively resist the behaviours which hegemonic masculinity personifies. Many men recognise they are emotionally and mentally damaged by trying to always be stoical, strong, inexpressive – powerful. Many men have little or no power at all in society. And it is very difficult to find an exemplar of hegemonic masculinity. In the past it might have been typified by John Wayne, Mike Tyson and General Patton. But was it ever clearly exemplified by Cary Grant, Pele, John F Kennedy, Nelson Mandela or Mohammed Ali?[45]

What hegemonic masculinity does is alert us to the fact that men of whatever race, ethnicity, religion or culture may strive for power and dominance over women and other men, and even though they may never achieve it, there is always the element of competition, of wanting to be one up on the other guy. This macho behaviour is embedded in so many societies and cultures that it is extremely hard to eradicate. It has come to define what it means to be a 'proper' man.

Secondly, hegemonic masculinity explains the pre-occupation, if not fear, that many straight men have towards the feminine, especially when expressed by gay men. Straight men will desire the feminine in order to possess it and gain pleasure from it, but most certainly do not want to be identified with it personally or culturally.

Thirdly, hegemonic masculinity creates emotional constipation in the man. He is not permitted, under this toxic regime, to express emotions other than those which traditionally correspond with maleness; he has to be stoical or aggressive, angry or withdrawn, unwilling to communicate or shouting at the top of his voice. He is unable to reflect on his deepest feelings; unwilling and fearful of delving into his true motives and desires. Hegemonic masculinity emotionally castrates a man even while it purports to pump up his libido.

Finally, hegemonic masculinity validates a man's physical strength. Men are built with muscles and are expected to be strong, along with all the behaviours which can arise from that. Therefore it can be no surprise if a dominant masculinity reinforces their sense of needing to express their physical power over others.

So what about the estimated 15% of males who are gay or bi – how do they relate to hegemonic masculinity? Sociologists have identified diverse gay masculinities operating in various locales, and these can include a version

[45]   Whitehead, S.M. (2001) *Men and Masculinities*. Cambridge: Polity. (Chapter 3)

of hegemonic masculinity. Gay men too can be bullies or violent and sexual abusers. However, for the most part, gays remain excluded from those male cultures which pursue hegemonic (toxic) masculinity, because for straight men with toxic masculinity, the gay man remains 'the other'; the antithesis of himself.[46]

Whether one wishes to the use the sociological term 'hegemonic masculinity' or the mainstream term 'toxic masculinity' in effect they refer to the same thing: males striving to be powerful, desiring to appear macho, wanting to look 'strong', behaving competitively, negatively, aggressively and often violently, while at the same time being unable to emotionally empathise with others nor recognise their own emotional vulnerability and dysfunctionality.

Externalising Toxic Masculinity

While gender sociologists have been researching masculinity for decades, it took one person who was definitely not a sociologist to unwittingly throw the problem open to the global gaze. That person was film mogul Harvey Weinstein. At time of writing, Weinstein has not been convicted of any offence, though he has been charged with rape.[47] More than 80 women in the film industry have made accusations of rape, sexual abuse and sexual harassment against him, some going back 30 years. Weinstein's exposure on 5 October 2017 by the *New York Times* and the *New Yorker* was the trigger. Within days, the fall of powerful men began. By early February 2018, the *New York Times* had recorded 71 men 'accused of sexual misconduct' and who had 'fallen from power' as a consequence. They included Kevin Spacey, Roger Ailes, Mark Halperin and Roy Price.

However, we need to go back a year, to 2016, to see the emergence of the term 'toxic masculinity' in the media. In October of that year, *The Representation Project* produced a short video titled *'How Toxic Masculinity Dominated 2016'*:

> *This has been a tumultuous year. Whether because of high-profile campus sexual assault cases, mass shootings and the harmful language used by the President-elect, these are all the result of a hyper-masculine culture that values traits such as dominance, aggression, and control, over empathy, care and compassion. The result is a culture of toxic masculinity that permeates society. Whether it's bullying others, demeaning or degrading women, or placing a value on money and power above all else, these ideas and expectations are dangerous and need to be addressed at the dinner table, in our local communities, and on the national stage.*[48]

---

[46] See Nardi, P. (2000) *Gay Masculinities*. Thousand Oaks: Sage.

[47] Harvey Weinstein was subsequently found guilty of rape in February 2020 and sentenced to 23 years in prison.

[48] http://therepresentationproject.org/2016-toxic-masculinity

In some respects, Harvey Weinstein's exposure reflected what was already emerging in the zeitgeist, at least in America. From the early noughties, the UK had experienced similar sexual abuse and harassment scandals by high-profile men, notably Jimmy Savile, the MP Cyril Smith, Gary Glitter and Rolf Harris, though no critical discussion emerged about their masculinity. For the most part, their abusive behaviour was simply put down to their paedophilic tendencies.

The moment paedophilia, male sexual harassment and a host of other lethal and harmful behaviours caught up with toxic masculinity and went global was 16 October 2017, when the #MeToo hashtag was born on Twitter by Alyssa Milano. A year later and the world had changed and it is not going back to what it was. What has now emerged is a new gender consciousness in women that wasn't apparent even a few years ago. It is global and cuts across lines of class, race, ethnicity, nationality, religion and age. It is born out of anger and frustration at the behaviour of men. The recognition that this behaviour is not new but historic only serves to drive women's will to confront it, resist it and name it.

To recognise how men's toxic masculinity is expressed as practice is challenging, not least because while I have identified it under the generic heading 'aggressiveness', placing that as the primary impulse, in reality that impulse can manifest itself in any number of ways. Here are the main ones:

- Bullying
- Racism
- Physical Violence
- Verbal Violence
- Physical Abuse
- Verbal Abuse
- Repeated Threatening Behaviour
- Misogyny
- Sexism
- Sexual Objectification
- Assault
- Harassment
- Homophobia
- Ritualised Male Bonding
- Male-Only Brotherhoods
- Machismo
- Rape
- Paedophilia

Clearly, toxic masculinity encompasses a wide range of behaviours and is not exclusive to any one class, sexuality, ethnicity or race. Some men who exhibit it will be vehemently anti-racist but also paedophiles and sex abusers. Other men may be anti-racist, but verbally violent and bullying towards people. Lots of men with toxic masculinity may simply enjoy being members of a men-only brotherhood, not violent at all but ignorant of how their masculine practice feeds into sexism and, ultimately, misogyny. Some will be boys and teenagers searching for peer approval, thereby leading them to conform to toxic masculine behaviours – even if so doing damages their life possibilities. Toxic masculinity can be further linked to drinking cultures which not only reduce male inhibitions but strengthen male bonding and sexist behaviour.

The externalisation of toxic masculinity is where men's individual practice visibly impacts on an individual and on society. The moment an aggressive act is committed by a man we can see toxic masculinity in action. It is not difficult to identify toxic masculinity when it expressed as random shootings by men in America, men attacking children with knives in Chinese kindergartens, or male jailers committing atrocities against prisoners in a Syrian prison.

Nor is it difficult to equate toxic masculinity with the fact that, worldwide, over one third (35%) of women who have been in a relationship report experiencing some form of physical and/or sexual violence by their intimate partner in their lifetime.[49] Millions of women are at risk of death and injury from men on a daily basis. Indeed, based on the global evidence, it is reasonable to assume that perhaps 70% of women will experience a pattern of repeated abuse from a male partner at some point in their lives. The United Nations recently reported that an average of 137 women a day are killed by their partner or family member. Of the 87,000 women killed in 2017, half were reported as dying at the hands of those closest to them. In the UK, 76% of the 139 women killed by men in 2017 knew their killer.[50] This data confirms something gender sociologists have long known; "that the home is the most likely place for a woman to be killed".[51]

Raneem (19) met Janbaz (20) when they were both studying at Solihull College, Birmingham, UK. She (Raneem) quickly fell in love with the swarthy, handsome young man from Afghanistan. They married in a Muslim ceremony a year later. Within weeks of the marriage Janbaz was being abusive to Raneem, threatening to kill her if she ever left him. However, when Raneem discovered

[49] https://www.unwomen.org/en/what-we-do/ending-violence-against-women/facts-and-figures

[50] https://www.theguardian.com/uk-news/2018/dec/18/femicide-in-uk-76-of-women-killed-by-men-in-2017-knew-their-killer

[51] https://www.shethepeople.tv/top-stories/home-likely-place-woman-killed

her husband had a secret wife and children in Afghanistan, she did leave, in July 2017. His threats towards her then became more terrifying and she applied for a non-molestation order against him. Janbaz flouted that order and spent two days hunting for his ex-wife. He eventually found her, at her mother's home, on 27 August. He attacked Raneem, stabbing her twice in the chest; when her mother tried to save her daughter, Janbaz stabbed her too. In December, 2018, Janbaz was sentenced to life imprisonment for double murder.[52]

This is just one tragic and terrifying example of the externalisation of toxic masculinity in relationships. And it is an example that gets repeated every single day in every single country.

But we also need to recognise how toxic masculinity informs our everyday world: organisational cultures, leadership and management practices, sports fandom, social media, politics and educational under-achievement, and how it gets strengthened by ideologies promoting racial, sexual and national superiority.

Toxic masculinity is so engrained in society that we interpret it as a 'progressive act' when urban planners start focusing on how to design cities so as to make the streets safer for women, enabling them feel more secure when moving around a city. We applaud when trains and subway cars start having 'women only' carriages. We consider it a sensible move when cities such as Seoul find it necessary to introduce women-only taxis. And we look with some incredulity when a quarter of a million Japanese women feel it necessary to download an app designed to stop men groping them on rush-hour trains. This is how bad it is. So bad we have stopped seeing it. A terrible indictment of modern man and for which every man should feel some shame and take responsibility for seeing it doesn't continue.

The unpleasant reality is that global society is infested with toxic masculinity to the extent that it has become the primary definer of human society.

Recognising toxic masculinity when it does get externalised is, however, becoming easier. For the first time in human history there is a global critical conversation taking place about men and their masculinities, something unthinkable just a few years ago. We are now making the crucial connection between masculinity and violence. We are awake to it. The MeToo movement is a key aid to this process, enabling women around the world to speak out and identify male abusers, rapists, bullies and harassers.

That conversation is the essential beginning. But it is not the end by any means. We need to look beyond the physical and verbal expressions of toxic masculinity and into how the virus gets internalised in men's brains.

---

[52]   https://www.bbc.com/news/uk-england-birmingham-46017400

Internalising Toxic Masculinity

Long before Stephen Paddock went to the Mandalay Hotel on the Las Vegas strip on 1 October 2017, aimed his .223-caliber AR-15-type semi-automatic rifle at Harvest Music Festival concertgoers, and shot dead 58 people and left another 851 injured, he had fully internalised toxic masculinity.[53] We know this because his actions are inexplicable. They are those of an angry, confused and emotionally dysfunctional man. But a man sane, rational and determined enough to have spent months preparing for this moment; planning the slaughter of many people with the intention of killing himself at the end of it. Toxic masculinity is, in such cases, motive enough. Any other motive – e.g. racism, money worries, social isolation, divorce, misogyny – is just peripheral, an 'excuse' to vent the hatred that already festers within the man. There can be no rational justification for such an act. Toxic masculinity is the only explanation we need.

But what drives toxic masculinity to take root in a man's brain? There will be numerous answers but most will come back to power; the desire to acquire it, the fear of losing it or the need to hold on to it. And of course behind the power issue is the ever-present question of identity; a male requiring validation of his manliness, a masculine subject in search of the ever-elusive masculine in himself. A man in fear of who he might be and forever dissatisfied with who he thinks he is.

One very clear but tragic result of men internalising toxic masculinity is depression and suicidal feelings. Suicide has, for some years now, been the leading cause of death in UK men under 50 years of age. In Australia, men are three times more likely to die from suicide than women and four times more likely in Russia and Argentina. World Health Organization data reveals that 40% of countries have more than 15 suicide deaths per 100,000 men; only 1.5% show a rate that high for women.[54]

Mike was always a man's man. He was born into a London (East End) family that was led by a father who encouraged all the laddish behaviours in his son; drinking, sport, lots of girlfriends, fancy cars and ambition; playing hard, working hard. What Mike never learned to do was reveal his feelings, show his emotions. By the time he was 35 he had, on the surface, the 'perfect life': loving wife, two small children, lots of mates, and high-flying career as a successful financial advisor. "I felt I had to be one of the lads to fit in. But in the end, it did me in. I had suffered bouts of depression and anxiety while at university, but reckoned I could get over it. But I was kidding myself. Then I got promoted at work but handed a lot more pressure, one of my kids got taken ill and suddenly I was bottling up all this emotional stuff. I felt stressed

[53] https://en.wikipedia.org/wiki/Stephen_Paddock

[54] http://www.bbc.com/future/story/20190313-why-more-men-kill-themselves-than-women

and adrift but couldn't admit it to anyone. I never really believed in myself, it was all just an act. Trying to always 'man up' was actually killing me. I started drinking more, doing some drugs, staying out at night with my pals, coming home in the early hours. By the time I finally faced up to my depressive state, my marriage was almost over. I remember the first time I went for therapy. I just cried my eyes out. For me, therapy had always been a dirty word. But in the end, it saved my life."

Invariably, the process of internalising and conforming to toxic masculinity starts early, certainly before adulthood.

Early adolescents' (boys and girls) conformity to traditional masculinity (at middle school) links with depressive symptoms and academic engagement… One developmental milestone for early adolescents is the need to develop a shared social identity with one's peers. This development brings with it a collective conformity to specific masculine scripts.[55]

The medium through which toxic masculinity inculcates the subjectivities of males is language. Language is a central definer of the self and consequently has serious political dimensions attached to it. When young males are told "boys will be boys"; that "boys don't cry"; that it is important to "man up" and "don't be a sissie", they are being fed the discourse of toxic masculinity. They are being infected by a way of thinking and self-identification which pardons, if not lauds, their aggression, emotional distancing and sexual violations, and renders their subjectivity separate from that of the female. This is the drive which forces them to seek male identity validation through a hegemonic masculine culture of compulsory heterosexuality, male honour and pride, and ultimately leads to the subordination of women. This in turn creates a masculinist culture which feeds and translates into university hazing rituals, date rape, sexual assault, attempted rape, bullying, homophobia and misogyny and emotional repression. Recognising this fact makes everyone responsible, especially the parents.

Accountability is not just about taking the famous wrong-doers to court. It's about identifying and stopping toxic masculinity at our kitchen tables.[56]

The desire to be accepted by one's peers is a central force behind the internalisation of toxic masculinity. It can drive gay men to want to appear straight, straight men to sexually abuse women and hundreds of thousands of men to suicide.

[55] Rogers, A. A., DeLay, D. and Martin, C.L. (2017) 'Traditional Masculinity During Middle School Transition: Associations with Depressive Symptoms and Academic Engagement', *Journal of Youth and Adolescence,* 46:4, pp. 709-724.

[56] https://rewire.news/article/2018/09/21/im-a-doctor-for-teenagers-attempted-rape-is-not-a-normal-part-of-teen-behavior

Anton is a 30-something former professional ice-hockey player who lives in Montreal. He is black and gay. Both his parents are highly religious and homophobic. Anton never felt able to come out as a gay man, and his sporting abilities meant that he was always surrounded by men exhibiting toxic masculinity. He was lauded as an athlete, but marginalised as a black man and as a gay. For years he pretended to be straight; "dressing in straight men's gear, going to strip clubs with my teammates, appearing to like girls, and drinking a lot. I was trying to perform masculinity like the others". This performance, driven by shame and fear, cost Anton his mental health and he succumbed to depression, eventually attempting suicide. Only after he came out as a gay man and began the journey of self-acceptance did he overcome the toxic masculinity which had effectively crushed him. "I had to learn to love myself. All parts of me, not just the bits that society valued the most."

Anton spent much of his early life terrified. Terrified of being exposed as a 'lesser man' than his peers. This is toxic masculinity internalised and emotionally felt as shame and disgust. Not until he was able to overcome this self-rejection could Anton move on and become the man he was always capable of being.

The stereotypes that have historically surrounded boys and men are now under question. They are increasingly recognised as falsehoods, myths, lies and fictions we tell ourselves. But they remain potent and there won't be a boy in the world to this day who is not exposed to them in some way or another.

If society claims that 'boys will be boys' when they behave badly, that same society invariably says 'men will be men' when they too behave badly; badly behaved boys growing into dangerous men. Overcoming this self-fulfilling prophecy is essential to reducing the likelihood of males internalising toxic masculinity. And that internalisation is evidenced by the following:

- Compulsive domination
- Inability to empathise
- Resentfulness
- Low emotional intelligence
- Addictive behaviour
- Quick and habitual anger
- Possessiveness
- Emotional illiteracy
- Obsessive identification through work
- Jealousy
- Victimhood
- Unreflectiveness
- Fear of showing weakness
- Inability to communicate
- Unwillingness to learn

- Fragile masculine pride
- Feelings of emasculation
- Negativity towards feminism and women's and LGBT+ rights

All the above traits have one thing in common: they indicate a lack of maturity. Any man with toxic masculinity will not be able to fully mature until he makes the journey out of that cave (see Chapter 10). My own research suggests that most men do not mature at least until their 40s, and many do not mature at all. They remain rooted to boyish pastimes, childhood memories and juvenile behaviours, often re-enacting episodes from their schooldays, especially those concerning rejection, shame, guilt, embarrassment and disappointment.

These men fail to adapt and develop. And what holds them back is the fear of doing so. To mature as an individual, one must be comfortable in one's skin and take emotional risks with one's identity. Toxic masculinity denies that possibility, the reason being that it is essentially an externally validated model of male identity. It requires, as in the example of Anton, not self-validation but external validation by other men and, to a lesser extent, by women. Anton was only able to overcome the imposed limitations of toxic masculinity once he began to love himself for who and what he was.

It is important here to recognise that while toxic masculinity desires the female, it does so primarily as an accompaniment, an adornment of the masculine ego. For most such men, the women in their lives are not the ones who validate their masculinity. It is other men who serve that role. We can see the importance of this in male brotherhoods, in male bonding rituals, in male-only environments, and in the culture of 'bromance', with increasing numbers of men admitting they prefer the company of their male friends to that of any woman.[57] This trend might be seen as a challenge to homophobic behaviour, but it can also be seen as further evidence of the erosion of intimacy between men and women.

The male who has internalised toxic masculinity has, in essence, denied himself the chance to become his own man. Instead, he is on a hopeless quest for a male myth, a masculine archetype, be it 'warrior', 'king', 'hero', 'adventurer', 'lover' or 'wizard'. As I examine in Chapter 9, this quest is all too often the result of the man's toxic relationship with his father.

Stephen Paddock was none of these archetypes, and he knew it. Every day of his existence only served to reinforce his isolation, his sense of failure, his acknowledgement that he was, in his own mind, a loser. He was living in a world where he had little self-worth. Eventually, the disconnection between how he saw himself and how he wanted others to see him was too much. He chose suicide, but not before a final, deadly kick at society.

---

[57] https://www.newsnation.in/lifestyle/sex-and-relationship/romantic-relationships-bromaces-men-prefer-over-romantic-relationship-reveals-study-article-207876.html

Incel: The Male Fundamentalist

Like most people, the first time I came across the term 'incel' was in April 2018. On Wednesday 25th April, newspaper reports revealed that the man accused of carrying out the Toronto van attack the day before, killing 10 and injuring 15, allegedly had links to 'involuntary celibate' online communities.[58]

The realisation that there were men out there, misogynistic, anti-feminist, right-wing, emotionally unhinged and full of self-loathing, was not new to me. What was new and disturbing was waking up to the fact that these men were out to kill people for no other reason than the fact no woman apparently wanted them.

Incels obsess over their own unattractiveness – dividing the world into alphas and betas, with betas just your average, frustrated idiot dude, and omegas, as the incels often call themselves, the lowest of the low, scorned by everyone – they then use that self-acceptance as an insulation. They feel this makes them untouchable in their quest for supremacy over sluts.[59]

The misogynistic mentality of the incel is not new. It didn't suddenly emerge in 2018. It has been around ever since men have. What is different today is that social media has provided a 'safe' space for such men to connect and mutually articulate what is in their heads. In effect, they have 'come out' as women haters. They no longer feel compelled to hide in shame, stay concealed or pretend to like women.

Women are the cause of our suffering. They are the ones who unjustly made our lives a living hell. We need to focus more on our hatred of women. Hatred is power.[60]

The twisted hatred that festers in the mind of an incel is the most extreme example of toxic masculinity to date. But their behaviour does have its own sour logic.

1. They are isolated and rejected through, as they see it, no fault of their own. Quite simply, no one wants them; they no longer fit into society; certainly they cannot find a woman to love them or desire them. This means they are ontologically adrift. Their desirability as men is reduced to zero. They have no emotional support.

---

[58] https://www.theguardian.com/world/2018/apr/24/toronto-van-attack-facebook-post-may-link-suspect-with-incel-group

[59] https://www.theguardian.com/world/2018/apr/25/raw-hatred-why-incel-movement-targets-terrorises-women

[60] https://www.newyorker.com/culture/cultural-comment/the-rage-of-the-incels

2. Having internalised toxic masculinity, they are then prone to externalising it through verbal and possibly physical violence. This enables them to reassert their masculine potency, which in turn reinforces their toxic masculine identity.

3. These men overcome the terror of isolation through use of social media. They quickly realise there are other men out there, also 'suffering' from the same issues and who have the same fears, angers and hatreds. By connecting with like-minded men, they can then claim to be a social movement; this gives them a spurious credibility, not least in the media.

4. Being involuntary celibate becomes its own self-fulfilling motif. It provides a rallying point, a name, an identification. These men overcome the humiliation of being undesirable by being unified; they unite around the label. Being a self-declared 'incel' not only gives an existential value to men who otherwise have little of value in their lives, it means they can have a voice. They instil fear in society; their rage, together with any random acts of violence, gives them a platform. They become a toxic brotherhood.

Whatever the typical incel feels about black men, gay men, handsome men, rich men, men who have lots of girlfriends, or simply men who are happily married and getting laid regularly, the primary focus of their hatred is women, and especially feminists and feminism. Their discourse is fundamentally misogynistic but also draws nourishment from white supremacy, fascism and the alt-right. Four years before the Toronto attack, self-confessed incel Elliot Rodger stabbed and shot six people in California. He left behind 'a 141-page manifesto expressing his frustrations over his virginity and his hatred of women'.[61] Another 'celebrity' of the incel community is mass-murderer Chris Harper-Lee: 'a reclusive figure, obsessed with Nazis and the IRA and without a girlfriend." Harper-Lee went on a shooting rampage at a college in Oregon in October 2015, killing 10 people. Other murderous men self-identifying as incels include Scott Beierle (two women murdered, five injured at a yoga studio in Florida) and George Sodini (killing spree at a fitness centre in Pennsylvania 'because of his struggles to find a girlfriend').[62]

For the vast majority of people confronted with the bizarre rationale and terrifying behaviour of the incel, it is like being plunged into a dystopian Margaret Atwood novel, with yourself as a reluctant participant. But are all

---

[61] https://www.nytimes.com/interactive/2014/05/25/us/shooting-document.html

[62] https://www.independent.co.uk/news/long_reads/incel-interview-sex-relationship-celibacy-romantic-rejections-community-a8626366.html

incels uneducated, unintelligent, lacking even a rudimentary understanding of civil values and codes of behaviour? Are they all monsters intent on the subjugation of women? No. And nor is every incel going to be dangerous and violent towards others. Many such men retreat into themselves. Indeed, a significant number of incels commit suicide. However, most will be externally aggressive and likely seek some solace from intense harassment campaigns of women – especially prominent ones – trolling and doxing of individuals.

One aspect of the incel psychology is their internalisation of limited notions of male beauty. There is a dominant discourse with incels that claims that their physical unattractiveness, maybe aligned with low income, means they cannot compete in what they imagine to be the Darwinian struggle to reproduce, to have sex and to find a woman who loves them.

Many incels claim to be the 'nice guy', the one who would treat their girlfriend like a princess if she could only overcome her biological obsession with physical attractiveness.

> *I have failed to be worthy in the female eyes, that's the main thing. Life has proven to me that because I look a certain way, no one likes me. That's a fact. You should know that everything is about looks, money and status, and don't try if you don't have it. Give up... I don't blame women, it's evolution. Women have to choose this way, they have to choose who can protect their children because they have this need to create, to reproduce. They have to choose carefully and the criteria is this... I'm not sex deprived, I'm love deprived. (Mo, self-confessed incel)[63]*

Mo is not unintelligent. He is currently completing a PhD in quantum physics in Leipzig, but he is decidedly limited in his understanding of the shift in the gender order. He lacks reflexivity and is emotionally immature. Feminism would help him understand better, though he now sees that as the arch enemy. Mo is probably beyond recovery unless, that is, he can change his sense of masculinity. Right now, he is unable to see how his very performance of masculinity is the problem.

The warped world of the incel is framed around a gender order that is fast disappearing. He sees the world through a biologically deterministic, Darwinian, gendered order but one which has subsequently tilted in favour of females, leaving men like him marooned in a world of male fundamentalism; directionless, purposeless, and angry, with only other incels to connect with. Incels like Mo are living out the macho male codes of yesteryear, an outdated Hollywood exemplar of gender relations, which makes them look sad. And it is leaving them lonely. Their masculine model is less Justin Trudeau, more

---

[63] https://www.independent.co.uk/news/long_reads/incel-interview-sex-relationship-celibacy-romantic-rejections-community-a8626366.html

John Wayne. Their isolation is wholly self-imposed and the tragedy is that they cannot see it. They have not been rejected because they are physically unattractive: they have been rejected because of how they think.

The incel has put women on a pedestal, but it is a pedestal most women don't want to be on. Not if it means them behaving like Stepford Wives or Barbie dolls. The incel rages against feminism, but in so doing totally fails to understand modern femininity. They cannot relate to women, other than seeing women as oppressors of men like themselves. This understanding of themselves as 'victims of feminism' creates a vast subjective gap between themselves and most women. It is a gap that cannot be bridged by treating women as 'princesses'.

Into this gap plunges male fundamentalism: an extreme version of toxic masculinity. That is, a belief in the natural supremacy of men and an inability to co-exist with those who do not share in the ideology. In that respect, male fundamentalism is like any fundamentalism; it is fed by its own ideology and invariably ends badly. During the past 24 months we have seen this ideology of hatred demonstrated not only by incels but also by ISIS, by the alt-right, and in places as geographically apart as Charlottesville USA and Christchurch NZ. Male fundamentalism is nourished by emotional dysfunctionality, and it is this lethal combination which brings us male rampage violence and the autogenic (self-generated) massacre that is so tragically common not only in America but many other parts of the world. From Hungerford to Sinasa, from Beijing to Utoya, the same patterns are apparent, regardless of any publicly declared motivation. Male fundamentalism thrives anywhere men form brotherhoods with the intention of reinforcing misogynistic patriarchal conditions, expressing their communal physicality, airing their sense of grievance and imposing their omnipresent sense of manliness.

Male fundamentalists such as the Las Vegas shooter Stephen Paddock experience an acute sense of powerlessness and they live with this sometimes for years before they snap. As I discussed in the previous chapter, power is unstable and insecure: not everyone can feel powerful and for many men the 21st century is definitely an age when they do not. They feel left behind by modern society. They do not fit. They are uprooted, emotionally adrift; they are the 'left behind' with no feeling of belonging. Indeed, society becomes their enemy. Their value system, attitude and whole approach to humanity has become lethal both for them and for us.

In effect, these men experience a critical and fatal disconnection between how they see themselves and how they imagine society sees them. Their masculine self-image may never have been very robust, but for whatever reason it crumbles. And in that moment the resentment, anger, frustration and hatred explode.

Although Paddock was one of the most lethal solo-mass shooters in American history, he was by no means unique. It is overwhelmingly men who undertake mass killings. Between 1987 and 2018, only 3 out of 102 mass shooters were female.[64]

The vast majority of males who have toxic masculinity will not go out and kill, maim, rape and abuse, but they definitely have the capacity to do so. The margin between how they think as men and how they may react violently, is distressingly thin. We have seen through history how men, once released from the strictures of dominant moral, legal and social codes, can quickly go on the rampage, and rape is invariably part of their arsenal of oppression and terror.

The Democratic Republic of the Congo, particularly the eastern region of the country, has been branded the rape capital of the world,[65] which is an onerous title to have, given the heavy competition from countries such as South Africa, Sudan, India, Afghanistan, Syria, Somalia, Saudi Arabia, Pakistan, Yemen and Nigeria. Even the United States makes it into the top 10 most dangerous countries for women in terms of rape, sexual harassment, coercion into sex and a lack of access to justice in rape cases.[66]

What is especially telling about rape and its close association to dominant ways of being a man, is the way it inevitably gets used as a weapon of war by men against women, and often against other men. This is nothing more than the expression of brutal male power; the need to feel powerful over others and to express that power through terror, humiliation, pain, sex and violence. As we have seen throughout history, it doesn't take much for your nice neighbourly man to turn into a rapine monster – all it needs are the right conditions:

Azra was married and had three children before the start of the war in Bosnia-Herzegovina (1992-1995):

These boys they were my neighbours. I remember them as young boys when we got married. One day he (the rapist) came to my house during the war and asked me to show him all the room in the house... He raped me. He beat me so I could not breathe, and he kicked me in the stomach.[67]

Ana lived in the Croatian town of Vukovar when the war broke out:

The rapists were people I knew. There were six of them... I had to watch what they did to my daughter and she had to watch what they did to me.[68]

---

[64]   https://www.statista.com/statistics/476445/mass-shootings-in-the-us-by-shooter-s-gender

[65]   https://edition.cnn.com/2011/11/24/world/africa/democratic-congo-rape/index.html

[66]   https://www.cbsnews.com/news/us-10-most-dangerous-country-for-women-thompson-reuters-survey-amid-metoo

[67]   https://srebrenica-genocide.blogspot.com/2010/12/systematic-rape-of-bosniak-womens.html

[68]   https://www.thejournal.ie/rape-vukovar-croatia-2078516-May2015

Crimes against humanity can be analysed as arising from racial, religious, ethnic, political, territorial, historic, cultural or tribal causes. They may simply arise out of a need to survive. But these crimes are always carried out by men. Sure, some women may sometimes collude, but it is men who invariably deliver.

In Chapter 6, I describe the three main types of men who are in relationships with women. One of these types is the 'resister'. I first identified male resisters 15 years ago, when I was researching emerging patterns of masculinity in response to new gender dynamics.[69] I predicted that although there would be an inevitable global shift in gender power towards women, I claimed this shift would not go unchallenged, especially by those men who cling on to a traditional but increasingly unwanted form of masculinity. The incel is just one of the more disturbing expressions of this resistance and we shouldn't expect him to disappear anytime soon.

Male fundamentalist attitudes linger just below the surface of many men's psyche, which makes the declaration by Andrea Dworkin that "all men are potential rapists" terrifyingly apposite. This suggests that for many men, all that stops them being killers and rapists are any sanctions imposed by their social environment.

A Crisis of Masculinity

Toxic masculinity emerges as a direct consequence of males' need for self-validation, something that males (and females) are always going to require. To expect males to stop seeking self-identification with the society around them is unrealistic. It will never happen. The drive for existential validation and ontological grounding are natural human impulses. We come into this world devoid of an identity and the rest of our time here is spent searching for, acquiring and developing one. Everything we do is ultimately orientated towards this single goal; whether it be love, marriage, sex, money, relationships, social status, conflict, a career, or simply writing a book.

In the past, men had clearly demarked avenues through which they might achieve a sense of being a 'man's man'. The sexual division of labour, the public and private divide, industrial work patterns – these all reinforced patriarchal conditions. And arising from these were openings whereby men could strive to 'be manly': educational opportunities, leadership and management, the armed forces, building ships, mining coal, the professions, even being a bus driver: all these activities and more like them were available to men and validated traditional masculinity. The societies of yesterday were arranged primarily for the benefit of men, not women. But that was yesterday. Very few men will live

---

[69] Whitehead, S. (2004) *The Many Faces of Men*. London: Arrow.

that existence today, even in developing countries. And those that do will risk being displaced by Artificial Intelligence; robots taking their jobs.

The future of men is going to be very different to their past. And if you look at ordinary men today, one can have a lot of sympathy for their predicament. Yes, it is a little scary.

So how are males going to find that masculine validation which seemed so easily achieved for their male ancestors? They are not going to find it in male dominated work environs, because they are in decline. They are not going to find it in educational achievement, because they are now seriously outperformed by females. They are not going to find it in marriage, because women are opting out of that arrangement. They are not going to find it in being fathers – women are opting out of that also, plus increasing numbers are getting pregnant without a male partner. Men nowadays are not even going to find it as seducers, because women too use Tinder.

The traditional-minded man with toxic masculinity has only two options: unlearn toxic masculinity or be marginalised by society.

The crisis of masculinity that was predicted by sociologists through the 1950s, 1970s and 1980s is now with us – but only in part. This crisis is not universal for all men. Many males are not in any state of existential crisis whatsoever. The 'crisis of masculinity' thesis too neatly generalises about men and fails to recognise the fact of multiple masculinities. Not all masculinities were in crisis fifty years ago and nor are they today. It is also important to recognise that fears of a 'male rabble, a threatening sub-stratum of society', and men in retreat from 'feminization and consumerism' have been a key theme of writings by and on men for centuries.[70]

I do believe there is a crisis of masculinity, but it is a *crisis of toxic masculinity*. And that is to be welcomed. Society needs to go through this process in order to help men change. Those men, such as the incel, who have invested in toxic masculinity are confronting a terrifying existential reality: they feel unwanted. And in that regard, they are correct. They aren't wanted. These men are very aware that they are living in the wrong era. Mentally and emotionally, they are living in the past, but physically they are living in the 21st century. They do not fit. They have become marginalised, and they sound what they are: frightened and displaced, male refugees from a world which started disappearing around 1960.

In other words, the gender changes we are experiencing today are less a crisis and more a necessary readjustment which society must undertake in respect of its values. Certainly, it is triggering negative and aggressive reactions in many men and the incel is but one example of male fundamentalism trying

---

[70] See Whitehead, S. M. (2002) *Men and Masculinities: Key Themes and New Directions.* Cambridge: Polity.

to fight back. But it is hopefully a process that cannot be halted, and nor should we fear it. It is, in my view, part of an historic civilising journey which humanity has begun, and as Steven Pinker's research shows, is already resulting in a positive change in behaviour and a heightening of human values.

Importantly, this social revolution it is configuring and enabling the emergence of a new way of being a man: progressive masculinity.

Chapter Four

Progressive Masculinity

When researching men and masculinities, one thing you quickly learn is that appearances and background can be deceptive. Men can change. Men are not a stereotype. What you find is not always what you'd expect.

David, 50, was born and raised in the inner city of Birmingham, UK. During his teenage years, he was a punk, and proud of it – headbanging to the sound of the Clash, Sex Pistols and Madness. His sense of being white working class shaped those early years, though not enough to deter him from going to university, where he studied History. At 6' 4" and close to 100 kg, David can be an imposing figure, muscular and upright, all topped with his skinhead buzzcut, which he maintains to this day. If you saw him working in his job, you'd be surprised to learn of his background. For he is the Principal of one of the world's leading international schools. His commitment to gender equality, child protection, LGBT+ rights, and women's empowerment is total and permeates the culture of the school. David is married with two children. He is currently studying for a PhD.

Adrian, 33, has never lived anywhere other than a small town in Pennsylvania. Occasionally he visits the big city of Allentown, to catch up with his two older sisters, though mostly he remains where he was born; a house he shares with his mother and father. He even has the same bedroom, still showing posters of Nirvana and Green Day on the wall. His work as a web-designer means he rarely has reason to travel far. Adrian was a virgin until the age of 27, his experience of sex being limited to some kissing and a fondle. For a while he thought he might be asexual. Then at the age of 30 he began a relationship with a woman 20 years older than himself; a divorcee with a grown-up son. That relationship lasted six months and enabled him to acquire confidence with women, learn about his sexuality and consequently embark on a series of relationships. He has no intention of getting married, at least for the foreseeable future. I asked him how he felt about Jordan Peterson, the Canadian psychologist who has said a lot about women, men and the "illusion of patriarchy". Adrian replied: "Yes, I've listened to a lot of his videos and his theories around psychology make some sense to me, but his ideas on women and equality are simply rubbish, a disgrace." Adrian is a secular feminist. His parents are traditional, conservative Christians.

Ken, 39, earns nothing. He is married with twin girls (7) and lives in an expensively rented condominium not far from Singapore's Changi Airport. How does he manage this? By the income earned from his high-flying executive wife, and his role as a full-time househusband. Ken is one of a growing number of Asian men who are dropping out of the corporate rat-race to concentrate on what they do best – being fathers and raising the next generation. Nothing in Ken's own family background prepared him for this. He is an only son, raised by a father who spent his life in the Singaporean army, rising to General, and a mother who never had paid work. In short, Ken grew up in a typical Asian male-breadwinner nuclear family. And when he left university, at the age of 25, with his MBA from the National University of Singapore, that was the life he too expected to follow. Ten years later, and his life is very different. I asked him if he feels emasculated: "Not at all. I love my life. The fact my wife earns what she does is great. We just realised it made more sense to swap roles. Lots of men can do this. They just need to let go of their male ego."

These are just three of the many men I've connected with in my gender work and research over 30 years and I place each of them under the label of 'progressive men'. That is, they have a performance of masculinity that is liberal, open, reflective and which embraces modern gender values. David, Adrian and Ken do have vast differences of experience in terms of life and relationships, but with regards to their masculinity they are brothers in arms.

I have met men like this all over the world. And you can find them everywhere. Sure, many are gay or bi, some are transsexual or transgendered, but the majority are straight. How these straight males somehow manage to negotiate their way out of the sexist, patriarchal cul-de-sac in which many of their male peers find themselves, is a major study in itself. My own research[71] suggests that a number of variables need to be operating in a straight man's life if he is to become a progressive man, if he is to articulate and be comfortable with a progressive masculinity.

Indicators of Progressive Masculinity

The 10 Primary Indicators

1. He does not feel threatened by women's power, or powerful women
2. Feminist: supports LGBT+ rights and the MeToo movement
3. Liberal-minded and open to alternative cultural expressions

---

[71] Whitehead, S.M., Talahite, A. and Moodley, R. (2013) *Gender and Identity*. Don Mills, Ont.: Oxford Univ. Press.

4. Anti-racist
5. Reflective, able to recognise and express his emotions positively
6. Negotiates and shares child-care duties with partner
7. Negotiates and shares household duties with partner (may be househusband)
8. Pro-choice (abortion and birth control)
9. Approaches intimate relationships from the standpoint of equality and equity
10. Masculinity not threatened by partners with higher professional status or earning power

The 10 Secondary indicators

1. College/university educated
2. Seeks personal improvement (emotionally and intellectually)
3. Ambitious but also aims for a good work-life balance
4. Not avidly following any single religion but possibly spiritual
5. Can articulate his feelings and thoughts
6. Not prone to outbursts of aggression or violence
7. Comfortable with new technology
8. Considers himself a global citizen with an international mindedness
9. Has developed emotional bonds and friendship networks with straight and gay men.

I consider the most critical variable to be the first; *the man is either a declared feminist or he is comfortable with, and therefore unthreatened by, the power that women are acquiring and expressing today.*

Following which, my personal criteria for being a feminist, of whatever sex or gender, is as follows:

If you believe in equality for women, are pro LGBT+, consider that all societies must challenge male abuse, and de facto, educate males into less violent and damaging forms of behaviour, then you are a feminist.

If a man cannot meet this benchmark then he is very likely to be still embracing toxic masculinity, at least to some degree. Any man who has become more entrenched in his anti-feminist stance and allowed it to spill over into misogynistic attitudes, including trolling, abuse and violence towards women and LGBT+ people, will have slipped into male fundamentalism. Not all men with toxic masculinity will become male fundamentalists, but all male fundamentalists will have toxic masculinity.

As I explore in Chapters 9 and 10, toxic masculinity can be unlearned, most typically by the man experiencing some emotional moment which forces him to confront and critique his long-held masculine assumptions and gender stereotypes. This often provides the man with the impetus to leave his toxic cave. However, male fundamentalism will prove much more resistant and, in most cases, will require the interventions of a specialist counsellor.

Redesigning Masculinity

I am very clear that progressive masculinity is now so common and widespread as to be a distinguishable pattern within the global expressions of masculinity. At the same time, it is important to recognise that gender performance is highly variable, multiple and ultimately is the specific expression created and performed by an individual. In theory at least, there are potentially as many masculinities as there are men. Likewise, femininities and women. Also, there is significant cross-over between masculinities and femininities. As I stated in Chapter 2, these gender identifications are created by society, not by nature. And it is a society or a culture that defines what masculinity and femininity are considered to be. But neither society nor culture are stable. Consequently, we are dealing here with very fluid, contingent and unpredictable sets of definitions.

That said, what has changed over the past few decades are the social responses to feminism, liberalisation and globalisation. These conditions have coalesced to create new ways of thinking about women and about men, from which have emerged new patterns of identity and behaviour. In effect, the last fifty years have been a global journey in the redefinition of both femininity and masculinity, leading to the point that we can now see progressive masculinity as a dominant model and increasingly representative of men's behaviour. In short, certainly since the end of the Second World War, masculinity has been undergoing redesign, not just in the West but ultimately globally.

It began with Western women and a Western-defined feminism, and has quickly moved out through global societies like the ripples in a pond. Men like David, Adrian and Ken did not get there on their own. They did not create their progressive masculinity independently of society. At some stage on their life journey they were exposed to feminist ideas and values, engaged with those ideas, learned from them and in due course adapted their male behaviour in response. For whatever reason, they did not resist feminism, at least the essential value system with which feminism is aligned. This is the osmosis process that we all go through in acquiring a sense of our gender identity. It is no different for men than it is for women. The only differences lie in the discourses (codes, languages, behaviours, beliefs) which have come to be identified with one or the other sex. Feminism quite simply encapsulates a distinct set of discourses and these present a value system with which the individual can align and which resonates with that person's sense of self. Male fundamentalism presents a totally opposing discourse, primarily framed around the languages and practices of misogyny.

Once a critical mass of men emerge who are all saying, thinking and acting in a similar way, then we have a new form of masculinity. In the 21st century, globalisation and the information society speeds up this process of osmosis and dissemination to the extent that we now have progressive men performing progressive masculinity in every corner of the globe.

But do they represent the majority of men?

This is hard to answer, though I suspect not; at least not yet. A large number of cultures and countries are avidly and actively resisting progressive masculine values and performances, certainly when expressed as support for LGBT+ people and the emancipation of women. This in itself will not prevent individuals or groups of men in such locations from adopting a progressive masculine stance, but they will have to navigate some challenging resistance and negative attitudes first. Any male progressiveness will have to overcome traditional gender values in the mindsets of both the men and the womenfolk; very likely in their own family. Plus, the male fundamentalism that dominates in many countries will be an additionally inhibiting factor. Add in the religious ideology and the masculinist political culture, then one can expect that in most of Africa, Central and South America, the Middle East, Central Asia, Eastern Europe, and parts of Eastern Asia, any progressive male who emerges is a very strong man indeed; not only comfortable in himself, but also unburdened by traditional male ego syndrome.

Where I am confident one will find a majority of progressive men is in certain professions and certain locations. For example, from my experience they are the majority in education, both state and private, and are to be found in universities, colleges and similar organisations worldwide. For example, if you spend time in Western universities, or indeed any of the leading world universities and colleges, then you are more likely to find that progressive masculinity dominates, even while toxic masculinity may well be present to some degree. Feminism is now an established discourse in higher education regardless of the country. To be sure, you are more likely to find feminist men and women in a leading UK university than you would in some other parts of the world, but the trends are identical, which is towards more enlightened ways of thinking about gender, sex and sexual identities.

Reflections on a Journey

My own journey towards a more enlightened understanding of gender, sex and sexuality didn't really begin until I was 40 years of age. I was a late starter in many ways. I'd left school two weeks before my 15th birthday, gone straight into my family's small florist shop business in Southport, UK, and had no qualifications at all. It remained that way until my early 30s, when, encouraged by my success in amateur athletics coaching and running, I passed the exam to become a UK Senior Athletics Coach. That was my very first qualification of any description. From the age of 25 to my mid 30s my wife and I had been managers of pubs/restaurants in Yorkshire and that seemed my destiny. But events happened and my life path took an unexpected turn. I found myself doing part-time teaching of physical education at a secondary school in Leeds, and a year later I had a full-time lectureship at a Leeds Further Education College. It was 1987. The college encouraged me to do a part-time teacher training programme, on completion of which I began an MA in Sociology at Leeds Metropolitan University. I'd embarked on that MA solely with the intention of adding some academic credibility to my developing career as an FE college manager, but in fact it changed my life completely. One of the second-year options on the MA was 'feminist theory'. Although I'd developed some awareness of class and race issues in society, I was really unfamiliar with, and not a little wary of, feminism and feminists, who I saw as rather strident, severe and intimidating women. But something told me to do this option, and I did. The MA Director, Professor Sheila Scraton, was an established feminist academic, and it was under her guidance and encouragement that I tentatively ventured into the study of gender, both as theory and as practice. My thesis was on men and masculinities in sport. I got a Distinction for that and for the MA overall. By then it was August 1992 and I was 43. The next step was the risky one. Should I continue my momentum and pursue a PhD, or should I quit while I was ahead? Nothing in my past suggested I was capable of a doctorate and I didn't need one for my career. But I was increasingly immersed in feminism and especially the sociology of men and masculinities, which by then was slowly emerging as a distinct field within sociology. In March 1993, I took the plunge and went for the PhD, nervous, excited, but determined not to fail. The title was *'Public and Private Men: Masculinities at work in education management'*. I had two superb supervisors; Prof Sheila Scraton (LMU) and Prof Jeff Hearn (Manchester). The next three years were amazing, I enjoyed every moment of the study and the research. I realised I had found my destiny. In December 1996, I had my viva and was awarded a clear pass with no corrections required, upon which I became a Doctor of Philosophy. I believe my thesis is still in LMU library. Having established my academic credentials, I changed career once more, this time heading for Keele University where, in September 1997, I began a lectureship in Education. Aside from teaching and the occasional conference, my professional life thereafter was primarily devoted to writing about men and masculinities, gender and identity, and relationships. This is my twelfth book.

My very tentative initial steps into feminism had shifted from uncertainty into full-blooded engagement. I learned the different feminist theories, the philosophy, the politics, the practices and the contradictions within feminism. I learned that there is no such thing as a 'pure feminist'; ultimately, we are all human and while we may hold strong political and moral positions, inevitably all this must be negotiated with the world we live in. I read everything I could get my hands on, finally settling on my current intellectual position as a feminist poststructuralist, largely influenced by Foucault, Butler and the likes of Lyotard and Derrida. I became increasingly academically confident and, importantly, very aware of my own masculinity. No longer frightened of feminists, I became one. And have remained so to this day.

Did I ever have toxic masculinity? I believe so, certainly into my early 30s. However, I have never been a 'man's man' and even in childhood preferred to read books than kick a football. I have been anti-racist and certainly sensitive to social injustice since childhood. I remember my parents remarking that an aunt of mine, my mum's younger sister, was 'acting very modern' by wearing trousers. That was around 1955. The comment struck me as strange even then. I also recall talking to my secondary school teacher about racism in the USA and finding myself beginning to articulate feelings and positions which informed my feminism in later life. During the 1960s, I had several openly gay friends at a time when few gays risked coming out. That said, I had undoubtedly caught some of the masculinist attitudes of my father and of my post-war generation, tempered as they were by the more enlightened approach of my mother. My family seemed full of weak men and strong women, which is the reason why I have always been attracted to the latter.

One area that I did steer clear from during my PhD, and really into my mid 50s, was my heterosexuality. But that couldn't remain the case. I had to experiment, theorise and analyse, and so I did. That subsequently took me on a very interesting journey but one to be recorded, perhaps, another time. Only now, at the age of 70, can I look back on my gender and sexual history and see the ways in which background, society, culture, race, class, ethnicity, masculinity, femininity, power, identity, age and biology all conspired to lead me to where I was, where I am today, and very likely where I am heading.

Questioning Progressive Masculinity

Below are 23 questions which we should ask about progressive masculinity, together with my answers.

1. *Is this about men simply becoming feminine?* No. One has to stop thinking about masculine and feminine behaviours as biological, and that is implied in this question. Traits like violence, aggression,

empathy, emotional intelligence, compassion, trust and anger are not confined to any single sex. They transcend genitalia. What we have, therefore, are men being more comfortable in behaving in ways which society has defined as 'feminine'. This itself does not make men feminine, it just makes them more rounded.

2. *How is progressive masculinity linked to the civilising process?* If we take the 'civilising process' to mean global society becoming increasingly sensitised to violence in all its forms, considering it repugnant and no longer a suitable 'solution' for addressing conflict, either state or personal, then we can assume that society is challenging toxic masculinity both directly and indirectly, because it is within men and their masculinist cultures that violence flourishes and gets normalised as natural male behaviour. I believe this process had begun long before the term 'toxic masculinity' hit the headlines, very likely spurred on by the mass slaughter of the last century. Whatever the cause, there is now a deepening current within global society that rejects violent (male) behaviour and this certainly aligns with new forms of masculinity.

3. *Are men with progressive masculinity giving in – losing the gender war?* The question represents the ancient problem with straight men – that they too easily relate to women (and gays) in terms of conflict and domination. It is eradicating this mentality which is necessary if men are to move forward. Progressive masculinity is not about winning or losing any gender war; it is about harmony and togetherness. That said, as I state below, men who engage in progressive masculinity must be prepared to accept the end of any patriarchally driven power. They must give that up in order to become better men. Right now, this is the only form of masculinity which holds out any promise of togetherness with women. Both toxic masculinity and to some extent collapsed masculinity (described in Chapter 5) will result in men and women continuing to grow apart.

4. *Do all men with progressive masculinity see themselves as feminists?* No. 'Feminist' is a label which has, for decades, carried negative connotations, not only for men but also for many women. This is the consequence of the endless mindless critique by mainstream media. However, the rise of internet social media has largely reversed that trend, resulting in more men and women openly aligning with the identity 'feminist', the reason being that

social media has opened up the discourse of feminism to millions of women (and men) who would otherwise never directly encounter it and in so doing has helped 'normalise' the label 'feminist'. That said, large numbers of men who express progressive masculinity will not even think of themselves as feminists; they will simply see themselves as liberal minded males, a moral and ethical standpoint which encompasses anti-racism, anti-sexism and support for equal opportunities in all its forms.

5. *Does the rise of progressive masculinity correspond with a drop in male power?* Yes. But progressive masculinity is not the cause of this reduction in male power. That will happen whether or not men adopt progressive masculinity. The reason is the inevitable global rise of women. The idea that 50% of the population, plus LGBT+ people, could remain prisoners of hegemonic masculinity was always a non-starter. What we are witnessing at the beginning of the 21st century is an awakening, without doubt the most profound and far-reaching political revolution ever to be experienced by human society. As I stated in Chapter 2, this is a zero-sum power game, with men the inevitable losers. For women to acquire power, men will have to lose it. Why? Because male gender power relied on the subjugation of women. Once that subjugation disappears, so does the male gender power base. Progressive masculinity is simply the by-product of this process. Individual men will still have power, but so will individual women. The power balance will, hopefully, be more equitable.

6. *Are men with progressive masculinity simply 'Metrosexuals'.* Not entirely. Metrosexuality[72] is a useful term to describe some aspects of progressive masculinity, notably the changing attitudes that many men have towards work-life balance, personal hygiene, physical fitness, mental health, emotional management and appearance, but it does not in itself signal the liberalisation of masculinity away from toxic performances. In other words, while metrosexuality can reveal how men are becoming more comfortable with non-traditional forms of maleness, it doesn't tell us how such men feel about feminism, women's power, racism, etc.

7. *Is the rise in progressive masculinity linked to men losing testosterone?* As I discuss in Chapter 2, testosterone levels are not fixed in males – they can and do fluctuate depending on external

---

[72]   See Whitehead, Talahite and Moodley (2013) *Gender and Identity* (Chapter 11).

factors. In other words, behaviour (and environment) impacts on testosterone as much if not more than testosterone impacts on behaviour. There have been few if any longitudinal studies tracking testosterone levels among the same men. However, published medical research has revealed "substantial" drops in US men's testosterone levels since the 1980s. Similar reductions are evident in many countries. It appears to be related to sedentary lifestyles, poor health levels, poor diet and obesity rather than ageing or, indeed, masculinity.[73]

8. ***Can all men develop progressive masculinity?*** In theory, yes. In reality, no. For all men to adopt and perform progressive masculinity there would have to be a wholesale liberalisation of human values, not just away from violence, abuse, and rampant and avid economic competitiveness, but embracing a moral and ethical code which protects human society and individuals. This cannot be achieved independent of other factors, such as poverty, education, culture, corruption, drugs, crime, racism and a deteriorating environment. But there are ways of encouraging males to adopt progressive masculinity and these are outlined in Chapters 9 and 10.

9. ***What are the material benefits of having progressive masculinity?*** The most obvious benefit is that the male will be able to more easily fit into and contribute to society. That is, they will be much more likely to engage with education, achieve good results and go to university. This in turn will enhance their employment opportunities and their lifetime income. Males with a university degree and in full-time employment will be materially much more secure than those without either. In other words, men with progressive masculinity will be more employable than those without, and more able to progress in their careers. For those men who do not go on to higher education, then they too can benefit from having progressive masculinity, not least because it will open more opportunities for employment and career advancement and lessen the likelihood of them getting caught up in the criminal justice system.

10. ***What are the emotional benefits of having progressive masculinity?*** There are many, not least the ability to have equitable relationships with women and LGBT+ people, and enjoy non-competitive relationships with other straight men. In other words, to live in the real world rather than in self-imposed isolation or slipping

---

[73]   https://www.sciencedaily.com/releases/2012/06/120623144944.htm

into male fundamentalism. The criteria I have listed at the start of this chapter all point to certain positive emotional traits needing to be in place to some level within any guy exhibiting progressive masculinity; i.e. empathy, sincerity, understanding, self-awareness, emotional intelligence and reflexivity. Probably the two critical ones are empathy and emotional intelligence. Moreover, such a male will be less likely to invest in attitudes and behaviours which rely on the puffing up of his male ego, thus giving him a certain immunity to discourses of toxic masculinity. This combination of traits and behaviours goes a long way to ensuring the male has strong mental health, is less likely to succumb to depression and anxiety, has positive self-esteem and is therefore more likely to experience the world as welcoming rather than isolating.

11. ***What are the relationship benefits of having progressive masculinity?*** This is detailed in Chapter 6 but to summarise, the main benefit is that any relationship he has is likely to strengthen, not weaken, his sense of self. Having progressive masculinity won't guarantee a relationship lasts for a lifetime, but it will go a long way to ensuring that any relationship produces more positive than negative outcomes. It is more likely to end well, be healthy and beneficial for both parties, and, if it does go the distance, be a relationship built on love, understanding and companionship, not fear, hate, bitterness and regret. In short, progressive masculinity is the only masculinity which will stop or at least slow down, the global trend for women and men growing apart.

12. ***What are the benefits to a family of having a father with progressive masculinity?*** The obvious benefits are a greater level of harmony within the family; a more liberal open form of communication between family members; a hands-on and attentive father; a non-violent and non-abusive environment; and a family culture in which women and LGBT+ people are not treated as inferior beings but of equal value and importance. All these factors will contribute to children growing up gender aware, open-minded, and having higher levels of emotional intelligence. As I discuss in Chapters 9 and 10, fathers (absent or present) have a massive influence on their sons and this cannot be understated when looking at how toxic masculinity can be avoided or taken up by a male. Having a progressive masculine father won't guarantee his son doesn't end up with the TM virus, but it definitely makes it much less likely.

13. ***How can I learn progressive masculine behaviour?*** Your starting point must be to accept the fact that men are not superior to women in any way. If you can truly do this then you can move onto the next stage which is to demonstrate that in your everyday behaviour, including your language, which means treating women as you yourself would like to be treated and how you'd like your loved ones, male and female, to be treated. You do not need to become a declared feminist, but you should not feel threatened by feminism, plus you must accept its primary tenet, which is to believe in equality for women, be pro LGBT+, be non-racist, challenge male abuse and, de facto, educate or at least encourage males into less damaging and non-violent forms of behaviour.

14. ***At what age can a child learn progressive masculinity?*** As soon as the child is born. In fact, it can start in the womb, by the unborn baby simply listening to the sounds of life outside the womb, and that means gentle, soothing sounds; not yelling, threats and certainly not violence against the mother-to-be. If the parents are happy and content, the unborn child will pick up that signal and be likewise. From birth, the key objective must be to avoid slipping into gender stereotype with the child. Not easy to do, I know, but it is important for both males and females to grow up with positive self-image, surrounded by affection and feeling aspirational, regardless of their sex, but with strict boundaries for behaviour in terms of bullying, abusive, aggressive and discriminatory behaviour.

15. ***What can parents do to encourage progressive masculinity in their children?*** You have many options and opportunities and these are examined in Chapter 9. For example, you could start by giving your child a gender-neutral name. Or you might take it further, as did Canadian parents of 'Storm' in 2011, and not publicly reveal the child's sex/gender.[74] If that feels too extreme you can at least follow the example of the Massachusetts father who, in raising his children in a gender stereotype-free household, didn't flip when his five-year-old son decided he wanted to wear red nail polish at kindergarten. In effect, any action which serves to break down gender stereotypes will be effective, including choosing books which have heroines, avoiding gender biased language in the home, and definitely avoiding the pink/blue 'neurosexist bilge'[75]

[74]   See Whitehead, Talahite and Moodley, (2013) *Gender and Identity* (Introduction)

[75]   https://www.theguardian.com/commentisfree/2018/nov/18/not-all-pink-and-blue-when-its-comes-to-our-brains

which comes out of the mouths of some scientists. Oh, and if you are religious, just remind your children that "God is gender-fluid".

16. ***Can gay men exhibit progressive masculinity?*** It is not a given but it is definitely very likely. This is not to do with sexuality but entirely to do with the fact that gay men live in a world which still holds on to heterosexual normativity, and in many instances remains homophobic and even legislates against LGBT+ people. This living as the 'other' develops a social awareness in gay men which is beyond the imagination and certainly the experience, of heterosexuals. It is in living as the 'other' that one acquires a deeper appreciation of the depth of discriminatory practice. In other words, it is easier for a gay man to be a feminist and enlightened about gender than it is for a straight person. What can mitigate against this is when gay men are afraid to come out and instead adopt toxic masculine practices as a way of gaining straight male peer approval. But this is inauthentic and cannot be sustained without long-term mental health damage to the individual.

17. ***How is progressive masculinity linked to sexuality?*** This is discussed at length in Chapter 8, but the most important point to remember is that while masculinity is a social construction, sexuality is biological. Which means that a straight man with progressive masculinity is not bi or a closet gay. He is straight. But how he exhibits and practises his sexuality will very much depend on his particular masculinity. One would expect a man with progressive masculinity to not express his sexuality in any way which is abusive towards women.

18. ***If I am a man who enjoys watching porn, does this mean I don't have progressive masculinity?*** Feminists have been split on this question for decades and it is indeed, a subjective one, not objective. For me, I see no problem with porn so long as it is not expressed as violence or is paedophiliac. I know many men with progressive masculinity who enjoy watching porn and while it is a miserable substitute for a full-on sexual relationship, it is for many the only sexual outlet they have. In many instances it can also add spark to a relationship.

19. ***How can I tell if someone close to me, or whom I work with, has progressive masculinity?*** This is discussed in Chapter 6, but the first thing to look out for are some primary traits socially identified with females, empathy and emotional intelligence being the top

two. For me, it is inconceivable that any man with progressive masculinity could lack these two traits. You may find they are not apparent at all times and in all situations, but they will remain the base line traits informing the man's behaviour and attitude towards others. In other words, you won't find progressive masculinity in any guy who is hung up on being an alpha male, is racist, or who lacks compassion and understanding.

20. *If I experience a traumatic event might it affect whether I acquire or lose progressive masculinity?* Traumatic events can be life changing, which means they can be personality changing. If the event forces you to critically reflect then the likelihood is you'll become more emotionally aware as a result. This can well lead to you becoming more accommodating, more open and more accepting, all traits associated with progressive masculinity. If, however, the event pushes you into bitterness, anger, feelings of hatred and revenge, then toxic masculinity will emerge, pushing you further into the TM cave, feeding off your sense of injustice and isolation.

21. *Which professions am I most likely to find progressive masculinity as the dominant way of being a man?* Organisations and professions are themselves gendered and reflect if not propagate the values of their members. But organisational cultures can change, for the better and for the worse. It depends who the influential actors are and the historic culture of the organisation. If you are a man and you enter a masculinist 'total institution' (e.g. armed forces) then you can expect the system to try and knock any progressive masculinity out of you. Though as I discuss in Chapter 2, even the uniformed services are slowly becoming more socially progressive. If you work in education then you can anticipate a work culture that is liberal, progressive and LGBT+ friendly. Beyond that it is impossible to predict – which is why any man with progressive masculinity should do research on an organisation before joining it.

22. *Is progressive masculinity a social virus?* All masculinities and femininities are social viruses; they do not reflect a biological reality, only the ways in which societies and cultures have chosen to define and reinforce the male/female sex binary. Progressive masculinity merely reflects a more recent social virus which many men will pick up and exhibit in their practices and internalise in their subjectivities. As I explain in Chapter 2, this is how identity

comes into existence: It is not the product of a predictable set of biological determinants. It is the complex interaction of fluid social interpretations and the meanings we attach to language. It is useful to see all gender as being on the wind, not in the blood.

23. **If a man has progressive masculinity does that mean he is weak and soft?** No, it means the exact opposite. Any man with toxic masculinity is fundamentally weak and soft. He is in fear of female power. A man with collapsed masculinity (Chapter 5) is in retreat from toxic masculinity but may not have embraced female power. Only a man with progressive masculinity actually embraces female power. This makes him the emotionally robust and grounded of all the male types.

Chapter Five

Collapsed Masculinity

Many historians claim The Change began during the middle of the 21st century, though others point to seismic social shifts occurring long before then. Whatever, we know that by the end of that century humanity had ceased to reproduce itself and by 2120 the world population had declined to almost half its level of a century earlier. The global workforce was overwhelmingly robotic with few humans working more than 30 hours a week and a third not working at all, at least not in the way their ancestors had. The corporate world was dominated by a handful of global giants and the profit they generated was fed back into the population in the form of grants, basic income, health benefits, social welfare, life-long pensions and life-long learning programmes. This maintained the cycle of economic production and financial security to the satisfaction of the vast majority. It also allowed people the time to focus on self-actualisation; learning, artistic and creative endeavours. In 2125, the major powers had agreed to dismantle all their nuclear weapons. This wasn't as big a deal as was expected because there was no conflict anymore. The last war that most people living could remember was a minor affair, between the UK and Argentina over the Falklands. That had occurred in 2047 and lasted for just three months before being resolved by the UN in favour of Argentina. Violence had all but disappeared from society: globally, armed forces were reduced to 10% of their 2050 size with the financial savings being used to finally eradicate poverty; the primary role of police forces was to monitor and assist people rather than solving crime, of which there was little; religions had been required to rewrite their gospels in such a way as to preach total non-violence and all religious discourse was strictly monitored; hospitals did mental health checks of children from the age of 12 months to check for the presence of aggressive tendencies, and these continued, annually, for life; gun control was total, indeed most arms manufacturers had closed down; anyone who wanted to be a parent had to have a criminal background record check and be awarded a 'reproductive licence' by their local Social Harmony Committee; the few schools that were needed focused almost entirely on what it meant to be a 'global citizen', with EQ having long replaced IQ as the primary measure of achievement for all children; Educational Adjustment Centres operated in most countries and had replaced the need for prisons. Anyone with any aggressive indicators was tagged 24/7. While those living in the rural areas still hung on to some traditional values, for the vast majority of the world's population – those living in the 25 global mega-cities – life was uniform, relaxed, peaceful and predictable, one reason being that no one dared misbehave because the social credit system, introduced by China in 2018, had eventually been adopted by every country and sanctioned by the UN under its Human Rights Charter. Chemical drugs, manufactured under state licence and given out freely, replaced narcotics which helped eradicate the drug cartels. Physical reproduction was undertaken exclusively through Child Birth Clinics, with sex between humans being seen as a rather primitive, animalistic activity. There was no porn, no prostitution, no child sex abuse. Whatever a person desired they could have, but with a robot, not a human. This suited both sexes, because by the middle of the 21st century it was becoming evident that most people no longer wanted sex. It just wasn't compatible with their single lifestyles. There were no religious marriage ceremonies – these weren't banned, they just weren't wanted, though millions of singles did 'marry' their robot lover. Couples only got together if they wanted to reproduce, and few did. The emergence of single celibacy as a dominant lifestyle began in East Asia at the beginning of the 21st century, though it soon became apparent this was no cultural anomaly. Some gender theorists had been predicting the rise of the androgynist for decades, though few foresaw just how fast and complete the ensuing collapse of gender identities would be once it went global. However, for those that cared to look, the signs were evident before 2020; falling birth rates in developed countries, the emergence of feminoids in Asia; the rise of women, the growing popularity of robotic sex, the growth of the super solo society, and especially, the crisis of traditional masculinity – which was starting to be recognised as a mental health issue long before it was to lead to the complete collapse of masculinity in all but a few wild places.

Predictions

What I've presented above is my attempt at taking a current social (gender) trajectory and transforming it into a 'reality'. That said, it is risky for any social commentator, and especially any sociologist, to make predictions. I've read numerous books, mostly written during the last century, that predicted what life would be like today. No doubt you have also. Social forecasters nearly always get it wrong, sometimes embarrassingly so.

But we can and indeed should, observe trends, and in this chapter, I turn to something that is clearly more than a trend and certainly more than a hypothesis: the collapse of masculinity.

The above scenario is one possible outcome of the wholesale collapse of masculinity, at least when aligned with certain conditions. Accepting I've taken artistic licence with some of my predictions, many of the conditions and scenarios described above are already with us. While it is for you to decide whether or not you consider the picture I've painted to be an enticing one or a nightmare, what you cannot deny is that men are under pressure to change.

But changing into what?

One condition that will need to be in place if humankind it to emerge into anything remotely like the scenario described above, is the large-scale elimination of toxic masculinity. This would leave a gap which might get filled by progressive masculinity. If that were to happen, then it may well prove to be an attractive outcome for humanity and certainly an improvement on where we are today. Though personally, I don't believe progressive masculinity on its own could usher in the futuristic picture I have painted.

However, there is a third option; a way of being that has become increasingly visible over the past two decades, one that really does indicate the possibility of a revolution in male behaviour. I term this 'collapsed masculinity'. It is this masculinity, more than any other, which will lead to a world where gender performance is so blended in the population as to render the concepts of masculinity and femininity meaningless.

The Definition

Masculinity is an edifice, a social construction whose single role is to define and reinforce a political gender/sex/sexual binary. This has been an historic dynamic which for the most part went unnoticed, largely because it corresponded with popular ideas, beliefs and images of male and female, man and women. This is circular validation in action, when a myth validates what we imagine and thereby gets endlessly repeated to the point that it appears real. However, once these popular notions get exposed as myths, not least through the emergence of alternative expressions of masculinity and femininity, then the whole gender edifice collapses.

Today we are at that point when the core of the masculine myth can no longer hold in the face of its many tensions, contradictions and inconsistencies. This social pressure on the myth of masculinity ensures the edifice collapses and cannot be rebuilt. Masculinity has collapsed. Once we have that situation then we no longer have gender binary.

But for the moment, let me define collapsed masculinity:

Collapsed masculinity results from the inability, or unwillingness, of men to continue contributing to the myths which have historically sustained notions of traditional manliness. Collapsed masculinity infers an implosion, wherein the edifice of maleness and all supporting imagery is revealed to be an artifice; a linguistic trickery which has long influenced the behaviours of men but is subsequently recognised as being artificial and inauthentic.

The fact of collapsed masculinity is evidenced from two distinct but related shifts in the behaviour of millions of men. The first is the emergence of the Feminoid, the second is the emergence of the Retreater.

The Feminoid: An Asian Experiment

In 2006, the Japanese social commentator Maki Fukasawi coined the term 'Herbivore Men' to describe a new type of male in Japanese society. These men were "feminised", had "lost their manliness", were unaggressive and, for the most part, apparently uninterested in sexual encounters with women.[76] They were also increasing in number, to the point that by 2010, the 'herbivore man' had gone mainstream, eventually being described as "an epochal event in the history of the male gender in Japan". These males were not gay, and nor were they asexual. They appeared to occupy a distinct and newly arisen space in Japanese gender identities, a form of masculinity that not only rejected the militaristic and salarymen masculinities of their forefathers, but was reinventing what it meant to be male, to be a man; a reinvention that was explicitly physical as well as emotional:

On today's [university] campuses there are male students who dye their hair blonde and wear long skirts. Just the other day, for example, one of the young men who came to me to ask a question after my lecture had fastened his loose black bangs with a big red hairpin like a schoolgirl.

I think more and more [Japanese] men are becoming interested in wearing bras. Since we launched the men's bra, we've been getting feedback from customers saying 'wow, we'd been waiting for this for such a long time'.[77]

What began in Japan at the start of this century as just another example of the Japanese ability to surprise the rest of the world with its quirkiness, has proved more than resilient. The herbivore man was eventually accompanied by a new term, 'the grass eater', though the two in effect mean the same thing: a masculinity that has, in essence, become feminised to the point that it

---

[76] Morioka, M. (2013) 'A Phenomenological Study of "Herbivore Men" in *The Review of Life Studies*. Vol 4:, Sept. 2013, pp.1-20.

[77] ibid

disappears – it is no longer the polar opposite of femininity because it has co-opted itself into femininity.

My own term for this identity is the feminoid: defined as a straight male who has chosen to take on a feminine appearance and expresses himself in ways which have been historically associated with females (gentleness, passivity, non-aggression, docility, caring), but who is not experiencing gender dis-associative behaviour syndrome, or gender dysphoria.

The pulling power of this identity in Japanese society is revealed by numerous surveys undertaken since 2006 which suggest that up to 60-70% of Japanese men are now identifying as 'herbivore'.[78] Similar surveys reveal the lack of sexual interest that such men have, with over 40% of Japanese males in their 20s still being virgins and never having experienced a romantic relationship, and other reports showing anywhere between 18% and 50% Japanese men aged 16-49 'having little or no interest in sex.'[79]

The lack of sexual interest presented by the feminoid has caused concern in Japanese society not least because it is often cited as being the reason behind the falling birth rate. Whether or not this is the case, there is no doubt that many Japanese men's lack of interest in sex, together with the decline in marriage rates and fertility rates, and the rise of the 'super solo society', are not doing much to increase the number of Japanese in the world.

On the plus side, Japanese masculinity is, today, a lot less aggressive than it used to be. Between 1955 and 2000, the number of Japanese men arrested for murder declined by 90%, with much of this decline being attributed to the changing behaviour of men in their early twenties.

The fact that [globally] it is men in their twenties who commit the most murders, a notable feature of crime statistics, no longer holds true in Japan… this is something unique to this country.'[80]

This decline in Japanese male violence certainly appears a consequence of the emergence of the feminoid. Indeed, it is little surprise that commentators and researchers are now describing this as 'soft masculinity'. At the same time, like all modern societies, there is more than one masculinity operating in Japan. For example, there are (usually older) Japanese men who remain deeply rooted to hegemonic (toxic) masculine values. Likewise, there are those who reject both the non-sexuality of the herbivore male and the misogyny of the toxic man, leading them to express progressive masculinity.

---

[78]   https://www.researchgate.net/publication/305472063_Matters_of_the_Flesh_Japanese_ Herbivore_Men_and_the_Asexuality_Umbrella

[79]   http://www.menstuff.org/issues/byissue/herbivore.html

[80]   See Morioka, (2013)

As I explained in Chapter 2, masculinities are like viruses. One cannot control their spread once they are out 'on the wind'. And 'soft, herbivore, grass-eater' masculinity has been out on the wind now for over a decade. In which case it should come as no surprise to find it emerging elsewhere in Asia; e.g. South Korea, Taiwan, Hong Kong and China.

> In the Chinese context, 'meng' can be used to describe a range of things: from children's expressions to President Xi Jinping's new hairstyle. Notably, it is increasingly being used to describe loveliness in men. When a man is referred to as 'meng', there is a (positive) implication of femininity. The popularity of 'meng' in China, on the whole, represents a growing convergence among East Asian countries... The 'softness' of Pan-Asian soft masculinity also lies in its more sensitive and caring attitude toward women. The 'Herbivore Man' in Japan and South Korea, and 'Warm Man' in China, are all in line with this type of sensitive new guy.[81]

'Warm', 'sensitive', 'caring', non-aggressive', 'soft', and definitely not threatening to women: who said men cannot change for the better? The evidence for men being able to change, and indeed change into a model of masculinity which is not going to get them or someone else killed, seems a positive step and one to benefit all humanity. Or to put it another way, which type of guy would you rather have as a neighbour: toxic man or soft man?

However, not everyone is happy with the outcome of this Asian experiment in men and masculinity:

> These herbivore men don't connect with others, they don't have their own families or have children and don't really contribute anything meaningful to society, either tangibly or intangibly. They are like parasites who often live with their parents. So you can imagine how it is going to affect society in the long run, socially and economically.[82]

This quote from Dr Paul Wai-Chang of University of Hong Kong, is in response to the evidence which shows the feminoid to be now well and truly settled in Hong Kong. In other words, this is no longer an anomaly of Japanese culture, but has spread out across East and South East Asia, and extremely quickly. However, while Wai-Chiang is referring to feminoids (herbivore men) in reality it is not feminoids who are the men most likely to live the life he is describing; that is, isolated, removed from social connections and not 'contributing' to society. Some feminoids will be married or in romantic relationships, a reasonable percentage will have children, and most will be in regular paid work. Not all feminoids are virgins and uninterested in women.

[81] https://www.eastasiaforum.org/2016/07/26/changing-masculinities-in-east-asian-pop-culture

[82] https://www.scmp.com/lifestyle/families/article/2147743/how-herbivores-hermits-and-stay-home-men-are-leaving-generation

Wai-Chang has made the error which many commentators have made when examining this phenomenon, which is to conflate two different expressions of masculinity under the single descriptor of 'herbivore man'. What he is actually describing is the Soloist.

The Soloist: Self-imposed Isolation

Throughout history there have been individuals who sought total isolation from everyone else. We used to call them hermits. Some went into religious exile and went off into the mountains, and some just tramped the countryside. Today, in Japan, there are over a million of them, with some estimates as high as 1.5 million; referred to as hikikomori, the vast majority (75%) are young men.[83] Hikikomori is defined as a person who:

1.   Mainly stays at home
2.   Cannot or does not engage in social activities such as school or work
3.   Has continued in this state for more than 6 months
4.   Has no close friends
5.   Has no apparent physical pathology to account for the symptoms

While this phenomenon was first noticed in Japan in the 1990s, and was originally seen as yet another consequence of Japanese culture, cases have now been found in the USA, India, Australia, Morocco, Oman, Spain, Italy, South Korea, Finland and France.[84] I have personal experience of this phenomenon in the UK. In other words, this is not just down to the variables of Japanese culture and its recent economic and social history; this is a global phenomenon increasingly impacting on men everywhere.

Accepting that there are numerous ways of classifying this condition and indeed, labelling it a mental health issue, my intention is to focus on the fact that it overwhelmingly affects young men. For me, this is ultimately an identity issue and one which connects with men who are attempting to find a masculine space in society, a space which will validate their sense of being men, at least under the traditional definition of 'a man'. For reasons which I explore in this chapter, that space, that opportunity for traditional masculine validation, is now removed or at the very least limited.

With some Japanese hikikomori now in their 40s, having spent two decades in self-imposed isolation from society, and more men expressing this condition daily, this way of being a 'non-man' is not going away.

[83]   https://psychology.wikia.org/wiki/Hikikomori

[84]   Suwa, M. and Suzuki, K. (2013) 'The phenomenon of "hikikomori" (social withdrawal) and the socio-cultural situation in Japan today', *Journal of Psychopathology*, 2013; 19; pp. 191-198

Might this become a worldwide problem?... We need to consider the possibility that the hikikomori phenomenon which emerged in Japan in the 1990s might be the first sign of a larger disturbance in modern society in general.[85]

I don't think there is any question that this is now a worldwide issue, but not one which is wholly the consequence of mental health problems in males, or indeed females. It is, rather, an entirely rational and reasonable reaction to the impossibility that more and more males (and females) now face in respect of them ever achieving any existential and ontological validation through the pursuit off, and immersion in, traditional gender binary activities; i.e. employment, education, marriage, parenting, careers and homebuilding. In other words, the material and ideological conditions which have sustained hegemonic (toxic) masculinity down the ages are no longer with us, at least not in any unquestioned way. In short, hikikomori is a sign of resistance to traditional masculinity, indeed to all dominant gender values.

In other words, this can only be considered a crisis of masculinity or a mental health issue if you consider that traditional masculinity itself to be unproblematic. Currently, many health professionals are interpreting this phenomenon as problematic; dysfunctional male behaviour out of kilter with how men should behave. But to do that they need a dominant masculine yardstick to measure against, and the one they are using is hegemonic (toxic) masculinity. Their yardstick is what is causing the problem in the first place.

The hikikomori is just one of the more extreme and therefore noticeable expressions of collapsed masculinity. For a male to intentionally decide to spend his life in his bedroom is neither healthy nor normal, but it is logical. If society offers you only a limited space to express your identity, and insists on you conforming to historic codes of masculinity in order to achieve that identity, but then removes both the physical opportunity and reduces the social desirability of such codes, then rejecting this offer makes a lot of sense. Pursuing social isolation is extreme but it is a way of men retaining some control over their existence, living on their terms, not that of the social order. In other words, the problem is not with the individual: it is with society.

But why do these males not retreat to toxic masculinity, as many do? I put this question to Jon, a Canadian 'soloist', aged 30, a virgin, and living life as a single man in Toronto.

Unlike the incels, I don't blame society or women for my fate as a 30 year old virgin. My childhood was to blame. My parents were to blame. In the end, no one is to blame. I was dealt a hand and I am responsible for how it plays out. I hold no anger towards women – they've always been kind to me. Women have given me opportunities throughout the years, and I was simply too

---

[85] ibid

fearful to take action. I wouldn't say I was pro-feminist and at one point I may have been anti-feminist, but that was probably because of the media I was watching (Peterson and others like him). But I met a feminist and she became a close friend, she showed me that feminists are not irrational, man-hating, unattractive women, but rational people with sound arguments.

Another soloist is Brian; aged 24, currently studying economics at a UK university. I asked him how he felt about women and being a man.

I first had sex when I was 17, still at college, but I was going through a lot of personal stuff at the time and the relationship fizzled out. I went on to university and in my first six months I met a much older woman and we had a brief thing going, but she was married and lived the other side of the country. I had a close woman friend at university, a Muslim, but we never had sex. I ended up spending a lot of my time on my own, not socialising. I was not into the boy's activity stuff that you get at university; drinking, drugs culture and all that. I just wanted to be on my own, read and write. In the end it was simpler to isolate myself rather than pretend to be a man I am not. But the pressure to conform became too much and I quit university at the end of my first year. I then spent the next two years basically in my bedroom, at home. Then I met a girl online, and we became friends. She has helped me get back to some sort of normality and I returned to university, to restart my studies, last year. Yes, I went through a phase of really hating women, blaming them for what seemed to be my pointless life, but I eventually I realised that the issue was not with women, it was in me.

Both Jon and Brian have had professional counselling for their mental health, their fear of the outside world, their inability or unwillingness to communicate, their almost desperate need to seek isolation.

To be sure, there will be instances when a man's behaviour is so extreme as to warrant medical intervention, but depression, feelings of suicide, low self-esteem and anxiety are not inevitably psychological problems which can always be diagnosed as a mental disorder. As I say, we should consider 'retreating' to be a perfectly rational response to a societal order that has irrevocably changed and in a very short time.

Males having to learn how to relate to females, and other men, has always been part of the journey of becoming an adult. When I was a teenager, the journey was not so complicated. I was married at the age of 21. My sister was married at the age of 19 and her husband was 20. They are still together. She has never had full time paid employment and her husband worked for the same company until his retirement one year ago. All my peers from my generation were married, in paid work, with most having children by the time they reached 25.

71

That world has vanished. And what has replaced it is isolation, singletons; a growing divide between the sexes. Some of this isolation is self-imposed, some of it arises out of fear of women, and some of it arises out of just insecurity and confusion. But it has one unmistakable consequence – collapsed masculinity.

What Has Caused Collapsed Masculinity?

During 2018, I conducted qualitative research into Thai women's perspectives on themselves, their relationships and their futures. The interviews were held Bangkok and involved 13 Thai women, aged 22-23. They were all middle class, graduates of leading Thai universities, including Chulalongkorn, Mahidol, Rangsit, and Thammassat. The interviews were conducted in English but with the assistance of a Thai female interpreter.

The women were all single and had already started out on careers including self-employment, marketing, administration, management, catering and modelling. All declared themselves to be straight.

When I asked "what are your priorities in life?", only one said "marriage and having children". Most said "career", "freedom", "money", and "quality of living"'. "Freedom" was the response given by most of the women.

When asked "what does success mean for you?", not one said a happy marriage and having children. The typical replies were "being independent", "happiness in work and life", "being rich and healthy", and "standing on my own two feet".

When asked "where do you see yourself in five years?", not one said getting married and having children. The typical replies were "own property", "build a new house for my parents", "establish my own company", and "travel everywhere I want".

When I asked "what is most important to your future?", not one said getting married and having children. The typical replies were "stable career with enough money", "money and looking after parents", "myself", and "good job".

When I asked "are you a feminist?" they all agreed they were, though they were also keen to state that they didn't see feminism as oppressing men, only that it meant "equality with men" and the "need for women to choose their own lives". One woman even declared that she expected to be the family breadwinner and would be happy for her partner to be a househusband. The dominant discourse coming from these 13 women speaks overwhelmingly of 'freedom', 'independence' and 'choice'. Not one of these women is expecting, or wanting, to rely on a man for validation of their feminine identity. Men are peripheral to their aspirations, not central.

If you want to look at what has caused the collapse of masculinity, then the answer lies with women like these. You may consider them rather materialistic and narcissistic, but there are countless millions more like them around the world, streaming out of universities: young, middle class, well educated, confident, and independent-minded. Sure, there are also many millions who are uneducated, poor, lack opportunity and are totally reliant on men for their future and prosperity, and many men who are insecure in their masculinity will gravitate towards this latter group ,not least because they will consider such vulnerable women easy to dominate, easy to attract and easy to get masculine validation from. But the future of women and men lies with highly educated, articulate and determined Millennial women, women unafraid to take on the label 'feminist'. These are the women who will very soon be wielding power and influence in society.

One further aspect of these women's identities is the rejection of traditional femininity. To understand why some men are now featuring collapsed masculinity in their behaviour, we need to recognise the changes taking place in women's subjectivities, and this I do in Chapter 10. Masculinity and femininity can only exist in a state of being mutually dependent on each other and that mutuality requires a discursive separation which posits male and female as fundamentally different. These are the two columns that create the binary, the gendered structure which has defined male and female identities down the ages, and those two columns rely on a continuing and very clear distinction between male and female. That distinction has broken down, globally. If it is happening in Thailand, one of the more conservative and traditional countries on the planet, then it is happening everywhere.

These 13 Thai women are not unique. On the contrary, they are typical Modern Asian Independent Women. In every core of their being – their lifestyle, their behaviours, their expectations, their aspirations – they are feminists. They have rejected traditional femininity. And in so doing, whether they realise it or not, they have rejected men who hold on to traditional masculinity. None of these women, if they get married at all, will marry a man who is not university educated and not supportive of their feminine independence. That would be unthinkable.

But these women didn't get there by themselves. They may think they have independence and agency but in reality they are a product of the age, just as the men are.

That age has brought massive changes for women, and with those changes have come opportunities that few women ever had in the past.

- Higher Education
- Contraception
- Globalisation
- Technology
- Social Media
- Post-industrialisation

Consequently, it is a lot easier to see where Modern Independent Woman is heading than it is to see where Traditional Man is heading.

Collapsed masculinity is collapsed precisely because it cannot exist under the reshaped gender conditions which are now apparent worldwide. To be sure, it has mental health factors attached to it, and we can interpret it as a rejection of and resistance to hegemonic (toxic) masculinity, but in truth, it doesn't stand for anything distinctive. It is a way of being (a man) that is wholly defined by what it is not; not by what it is, what it has, or what brings it power. Indeed, it is a way of being that does not acquire male power through its expression. This is what makes it collapsed.

Questioning Collapsed Masculinity
Below are 12 questions which we should ask about collapsed masculinity, together with my answers.

What are the key commonalities between the Feminoid and the Soloist? The most distinctive feature which is common to both is their unwillingness or inability to engage with and reproduce traditional masculine behaviours. I see this as a rejection of hegemonic masculine values and consequently also of toxic masculinity. This doesn't make all such men progressive, in that they are automatically aligned with feminist values and comfortable with women's power, but it does mean they are much less likely to be toxic in their masculine performance i.e. abusive, violent and aggressive.

Are all these men celibate? No, though one would expect celibacy to be a dominant trait within this group. Some feminoids will be in romantic relationships and some will be married but for the majority, sex is not something they are pursuing. Certainly the soloist, by definition, is not in any physical or romantic relationship.

Are these men afraid of women? No, not all. With feminoids one sees a desire to transform into a more feminine male and adopt feminine behaviours and appearances, though not in order to address gender dysphoria – so these men are not transsexuals or transgenders. With the soloist there may well be an underpinning insecurity, anxiety and fear of women, or certainly a confusion over whether or not they are 'man enough' to attract a female partner.

Have these men transformed into asexuals? No. Asexuality is a biological condition which is not likely to change through a person's life. There are relatively few asexuals in society; some estimates put it at less than 1%.[86]

Are these men gay? Some may be, but the vast majority will be straight.

---

[86]   Bogaert, A. F. (2012) *Understanding Asexuality*. New York: Rowman & Littlefield Publishers.

Can collapsed masculinity be reversed? Not through government intervention, though we are already seeing evidence of that being attempted in China, with increasing numbers of specialist schools having a declared mission to "train boys to be men". More on this in Chapters 9 and 10.

Is there evidence of women being attracted to men with collapsed masculinity? Yes. Ask most any Asian Generation Z and young Millennial woman the type of men she is attracted to, and the overwhelming response is the 'girly' men of South Korea and Japan. Not only are they seen as beautiful, they are seen as non-threatening.[87]

How similar is the Soloist to a toxic male who is isolating himself from society? The difference between the two is in their level of internalised aggression. I see the soloist in a state of harmony within himself, at least to some extent. Just because he has chosen to retreat from society doesn't make him a dysfunctional person. It is his choice. The toxic male, on the other hand, sees himself as a victim of feminism, a victim of women's growing power. He wants to put the clock back to a time when men's power went unchallenged. One commonality between the two is that they are both reacting to the demise of hegemonic (toxic) masculinity, the difference being that the soloist withdraws from society totally, while the toxic male festers in his own feelings of anger, hatred and frustration. Hikikomori are not a risk to society, while the toxic male is, certainly if he has graduated to male fundamentalism.

What do the Feminoid and Soloist represent? They represent one possible future of mankind. Whether or not you consider this to be utopian or a nightmare, there is no disputing the evidence. Both these male types are growing in number and becoming more widespread, cutting across religions, ethnic groups and nationalities. They also represent the demise of a form of masculinity, (call it traditional, hegemonic, toxic, or whatever) which has, to all extent, lost its existential purchase. Even if men wanted to pursue this masculine 'ideal', how do they? The social conditions which sustained it throughout history have now all but disappeared. All we are left with are the skeleton bones of male power, reduced to blatant sexism, discrimination, violence, abuse and misogyny. This is not power, it is oppression, which is why women around the world now speak out against 'the patriarchy'. The Emperor really is standing stark naked before us and it is not just women who see it. These men – the feminoid, the soloist – see it also. To be sure, their responses may be different, but they are both a consequence of the same global shift in the gender order.

---

[87] https://www.bbc.com/news/world-asia-42499809

How is Collapsed Masculinity similar to Progressive Masculinity? They are similar in that they both reject toxic masculinity. Many men can no longer live with toxic masculinity, it is no longer aspirational. They need alternatives. Collapsed masculinity is one outcome, progressive masculinity is the other. Which men will gravitate to which masculinity is difficult if not impossible to predict. Much will depend on their upbringing, their feelings about women and feminism, and the quality of their relationships with women and with gay men. Both collapsed masculinity and progressive masculinity are a big improvement on toxic masculinity – that is the masculinity which threatens society, in everything from male violence to the deteriorating environment.

Can a man change from one masculinity to another? Potentially yes, and this is one factor which makes it extremely difficult to confidently predict the future of men. I have had personal experience of men who've gone from collapsed masculinity to progressive masculinity. This is probably the most common conversion for men. I think any man who has fallen into male fundamentalism is unlikely to change without professional intervention. There are various shades of toxic masculinity and on the lighter side it is entirely possible for a man to start to accept women in a less hostile way, maybe even moving into progressive masculinity. Though again, his relationships with those women close to him will be a deciding factor. Another important variable is a man's sexuality (discussed in Chapter 8).

Which masculinity is most likely to lead to women and men growing apart, and which is most likely to lead to women and men coming together? That question is a big one and gets addressed in the next chapter.

Chapter Six

Resister, Retreater, Embracer

It is a truth universally acknowledged, that a single man in possession of a good fortune, must be in want of a wife.[88]

This is arguably one of the best opening lines to any book. When Jane Austen wrote it, at the beginning of the 19th century, it was universally true. Today, not.

No More Spinsters

The quote from *Pride and Prejudice* reveals the historic gender binary at work, and in favour of men. For centuries, spinsterhood was a condition to be avoided at all cost; a curse on a woman who needed a man for protection, and on a family that craved sons and heirs. To avoid that fate most women would settle for the first half-decent man who crossed their paths. Perhaps they'd get lucky in love. Perhaps not. Whatever, they persevered because the alternative was too awful to contemplate. Better to be miserably married than miserably single. At least a married woman could hope for the love of children to compensate for the fickleness of her husband.

The fact that you and I are here today is not the result of centuries of love and harmony between men and women, but centuries of hope, pain, bitterness and regret, all interspersed with reproductive sexual activity and not a little violence. In other words, more disappointment than delight.

And the world remains full of disappointed women. Most learn to hide it, or share their sadness with a few close women friends. Increasingly, however, women are just ignoring the marital option altogether.

The data on the global decline of marriage doesn't require repeating here. You'll already be familiar with it. But from a purely subjective perspective I can say that in my 70 years I have met very few women who have not experienced acute pain and disappointment in love. Some overcome their pain and remain married to the same man they fell in love with when they were young and dewy-eyed. However, the majority chose to exit, and onto divorce, serial

---

[88]   Austen, J. (1812) *Pride and Prejudice*. London: T. Egerton

relationships, new marriages, or just settling for being single and free. Given the overwhelming evidence that shows marriage to be a high-risk venture, with women in relationships at serious risk of violence from their partner, I find the singular optimism displayed by many women to be truly astonishing. And not just women in love, but women who are not in love but nevertheless remain expectant that 'The One' is waiting just around the corner, ready to usher in blissful lifelong happiness. To me, this seems a perverse and highly dangerous form of self-denial, one that most men, interestingly, do not appear to exhibit.

Whether you put this down to women and men being from different planets, driven by different desires, or simply and fundamentally incompatible, there is no denying the evidence. Women throughout history, and for both functional and emotional reasons, have persisted in apologising for their men, shielding their men, retaining faith in their men and loving them despite, not because of, their behaviour.

But that was mostly in the past, the days of Jane Austen. If there is one seismic social shift being felt at this point in history, it is that more and more women are disabusing themselves of the myths of happy ever after, and preparing to accept the reality.

Women are voting with their feet, or more aptly, shutting the door on men. And frankly it doesn't matter how much money the guy has, how big his car is, or how big anything else is he may possess; what matters a whole lot more is his masculinity, his sense of himself as a man.

One consequence of women applying a more careful and selective criteria to men, judging them not on traditional gender values of money, status and prestige but on qualities of empathy, emotional intelligence and gender awareness, is that a growing number of men are going to become 'incels', whether they like it or not. In short, they will never experience a relationship of any quality with any woman.

In my lifetime there has never been more noise about men and their masculinity as there is today, which is in itself quite extraordinary because throughout history there has been a deafening silence; male behaviour and its adverse consequences remaining socially invisible, protected by its very ubiquity. And when those first brave women did start shouting about 'equal opportunities' back in the last century, they were dismissed, marginalised and ridiculed; condemned as trouble makers or worse – feminists. Men went out of their way to discredit any woman who wanted, indeed expected, gender equality. And even those men who might be sympathetic to the cause invariably saw feminism as a 'woman's issue'. How times change. Feminism has gone global, mainstream, and taken root in every country. Now feminism is for men also.

Men have at last woken up to the fact that they have gender. Unfortunately, what they are now having to accept is that the gender they have may not be healthy, for them or anyone else.

What is telling is that so many men are taken aback at this unexpected change in their fortunes. They are shocked that women reject them. They are amazed at the sheer audacity of any woman to label them 'undesirable'. They find it incomprehensible to be, now, the ones left 'on the shelf'. And they seriously loath having their masculinity, their 'natural male instincts', put under critical scrutiny by women. Well, guys, welcome to the new gender order.

Did men really think that their gender power would continue unchallenged? Were they so dismissive of women that they failed to appreciate what would happen once that 50% of the population who had been previously marginalised, got educated, got aspirations, got confident and found a voice?

If women have been in denial about men's willingness and capacity to fulfil their romantic dreams, then so have men been in denial about the willingness and capacity of women to remain docile slaves to toxic masculinity.

The thing about myths is that they are vulnerable. It doesn't take a lot to prick the over-inflated balloon. And the men and masculinity balloon has been well and truly pricked.

Where has this left us?

For women, it has left them increasingly unable to find a partner worth investing time and emotional labour in. They are growing apart from men, reluctantly but inevitably. Sure, many women are finding true love and happiness, but many others are still compromising, settling for an 'okay' guy in order to be 'protected' and have a family, just as women did in Jane Austen's era. The only difference is that today increasing numbers of women don't feel the need to compromise at all. They don't need 'protecting'; they can protect themselves. If they cannot find a man who they can imagine spending the rest of their life with, they'll settle for singledom.

For men, it has left them with three dominant responses: they are either in resistance to this new reality, retreating from it or embracing it. These responses directly correlate with the three dominant patterns of masculinity discussed and identified in this book: Toxic, Progressive and Collapsed.

Toxic Masculinity: The Resister

In Chapter 2 I discussed 'power', describing it as an amorphous quality, largely invested in discourse. The reason why power is so important is because it is the key to unlocking men's masculinity; to understanding men and to understanding how men are responding, and will respond, to MeToo, toxic masculinity, feminism, women's rights, male violence and LGBT+ awareness – in fact, all the scrutiny they are now under. Ultimately these issues and trends, and others like them, touch directly on power, raising the question to what degree is man's identity invested in the notion of power over others, especially women?

Power comes from how we speak, what we speak of, what we are capable of speaking of, and how we present ourselves in the social world. Sure, power can also come from having material wealth and status, and power can come from threat, but in the final analysis all power must be continually worked at in order to be maintained. Physical threats will eventually wear off and wealth won't protect you if you act like an idiot, especially not today in a world where even relatively minor transgressions can get quickly magnified on social media and result in you having your authority seriously undermined. As we have seen in the past two years, even the very rich and powerful can and do lose power.

Power is always vulnerable, always under question. The reason is that it is always resisted; indeed, it brings with it an inevitable resistance. And that is especially true of gender power. Many women have resisted male power down the ages, though only now is that resistance emerging as a vocal, global force. Resistance to male power has now coalesced around feminism, and while different women will have different understandings of what that term means to them, there can be no denying the fact that women are asserting themselves, challenging men, like never before in the history of humankind.

However, male power is also about resistance to anything which threatens it, and the two biggest threats to male power are women rights and LGBT rights. As I explained in Chapter 2, gender power is a zero-sum game, so don't be surprised if men don't want to readily give it up.

To understand how the Resister operates in relationships you first need to understand the centrality of power to his way of being a man. Power is not just an interesting term which sociologists use to examine societies; having, maintaining and seeking power can be a reason to live. Indeed, power is what drives the ambitions of most of us: the power to be who we choose to be. That is the ultimate power.

Feminism, indeed even mild requests for 'equal opportunity', are about power. Whether they ask or demand, such requests seek change in the status quo. Any man who has invested his sense of manliness in the traditional gender order is today threatened. He may not feel physically threatened, but existentially he certainly is. If the momentum generated by 21st feminism continues as it is doing, then there is little doubt that more men will feel adrift. They will undergo the crisis of masculinity examined in Chapter 3.

Around the world we see men resisting women's rights and LGBT+ rights and increasingly more vocally, more openly, more stridently and more violently. Fear of losing power is driving this. In some countries such resistance is embedded in, and reinforced by, religious and judicial codes. In more liberal countries and cultures, the resistance may be more random, spasmodic and compartmentalised, but it still present.

In other words, the Resister is the most common response to the rise of women and contemporary feminist values, making the likelihood of any woman finding herself in a relationship with a Resister very high indeed.

The point to note is that any man with toxic masculinity will be a Resister to some extent, whether he accepts this or not. The key determinant of toxic masculinity is an inability or unwillingness to accept that women are equal to men, have equal power to men, should have equal opportunities to men and should be allowed to choose their own life path without interference from anyone else, man or woman. And not only women, but LGBT+ people also. If the man cannot accept this simple declaration, call it a Declaration of Gender Rights if you like, then he is locked into toxic masculine behaviour. Which means he is resisting – consciously or not.

The simplest way to discover if a man is resisting is to ask him this question: Do you believe in equal rights for women and LGBT+ people? Anything less than a 'Yes', suggests he feels his masculinity to be threatened by the question, notably by its implication that these 'other' identities are equal to his – and in every way.

If he responds negatively, or in a confused, defensive or uncertain way, you can be sure that he is having to internalise the question and having to deal with the sense of emasculation it engenders in him. In other words, does he feel emasculated by women and LGBT+ people having the same rights, the same power, as himself? Importantly, is he willing to forgo the power that men have held in society in order to bring equality into the world?

Below are 15 questions which should be asked about the Resister and my answers. From these you will be better able to ascertain the possibility of a man changing into something more progressive or retreating/resisting further and becoming a male fundamentalist, together with the chances of you being able to have a relationship with him.

What sort of physical behaviour would a Resister likely demonstrate in an intimate relationship? He is certainly more likely to be inclined to assert his physical dominance in a relationship. Whether this materialises as abuse and violence is impossible to predict without more information on the man and his history, but if the guy is holding on to ideas of male supremacy and women's inferiority, then it is not a big leap for him to defend that position physically, especially if he feels his masculinity questioned or threatened. This is a major reason why we have so much domestic violence globally. No country, culture or religion is immune from this. It is the most compelling evidence revealing the state of dominant masculinity and its continuingly toxic character. Some

Resisters will, however, not be physically threatening or abusive to their partners whatsoever, though they may well be with others outside the family circle.

What sort of emotional behaviour would a Resister likely demonstrate in an intimate relationship? Some Resisters will engage in strategic and relentless emotional bullying; others will simply be unable and/or unwilling to articulate their emotions. A commonality with all such men is their lack of empathy and their inability to recognise, interpret, accept and modify their emotional responses; most will not be good at intimate communication. They will be rooted into patterns of behaviour which have proved damaging both to them and to those close to them, but due to their low level of emotional intelligence they cannot stop this cycle and so it continues. Resisters can suffer extreme emotional trauma if they find themselves rejected by women; they are not good at coping on their own. Their lack of emotional self-awareness means they are vulnerable to depression, anxiety and feelings of anger and recrimination.

Can a feminist and a Resister have a good relationship? Many women feminists have found themselves in an intimate relationship with a man who rejects their ideas of female empowerment and equality. Indeed this is not an unusual situation, especially given the rise in feminist awareness among the global female population. I would hazard a guess that a majority of married women or those with male partners will today consider themselves equal to men, not subservient. However, the chances of their male partner agreeing with them are not high. Does this mean the relationship is doomed? No, not doomed, but it is living a lie; it is avoiding the question of equality in order to 'keep the peace'.

What if I love my guy, but he is sexist and homophobic? Assuming that you are neither sexist nor homophobic, then you are living a dangerous existence. You are with a Resister, one who is explicitly aligned with the core attitudes contained in toxic masculinity and who may well be exhibiting signs of male fundamentalism. You need to ask yourself what it is you love about this man. And don't imagine you can change him.

What if I love my guy, but he is racist? Unless you are a racist too, then my reply is the same as the one I've given as regards a guy who is sexist and homophobic. You are living a lie, pretending the relationship is sound when in fact it is anything but. Homophobia, sexism, racism, these are the 'canaries in the coal mine'. If they are present then you have a man who is embedded in toxic masculinity, if not male fundamentalism. They reveal the presence of aggressive if not violent attitudes towards 'others', and a male identity rooted in (white) male supremacy ideology.

Can Resisters Change for the better? Resisters who consider themselves to be materially 'successful' in life will find it harder to change; their 'self-made man' attitude only serves to reinforce their defensiveness and reduce their willingness to accept they are anything less than perfect. Resisters who have experienced emotional trauma (e.g. prison, PTSD, attempted suicide, addictions, bereavement) can, with help, move forward and use the experience as a springboard to recovering from toxic masculinity and exit the TM cave (see Chapter 9). Others may simply slide further into psychological decline, especially if they surround themselves with like-minded men. Much depends on whether they have support from enlightened and aware friends and family.

How can I make my guy less of a Resister and more Progressive? There is no general answer to this question as it all depends to what extent the guy is self-aware and open to questioning his attitudes, or whether he is afraid to do anything which undermines his sense of male potency. In other words, how much of a Resister is he? A general rule of thumb is that if the man is abusive and violent, behaving like a male fundamentalist, then he needs professional help. You cannot change him on your own. In fact, you may be at physical risk if you try. If, on the other hand, you and he can sit down calmly and discuss topics like women's rights, gender roles, toxic masculinity, feminism, LGBT+ rights and anti-racism, without getting into a full-blown fight, then you are heading in the right direction.

If I put the question about the Declaration of Gender Rights to my guy and he answers positively, how do I know he is telling the truth? Yes, many men will lie, deliberately telling you what they reckon you want to hear, but most will not be able to. At least, not with this question. It is too personal, too political. And if you have doubts, ask him how he'd feel if his son or daughter turned out to be LGBT? No Resister will be able to handle this question without revealing his deep-rooted prejudices.

Does it matter if I am a woman and my boss is a man Resister? Yes it matters, and quite a lot, especially if you are ambitious within the organisation. Corporations, commerce, business, the professions and every job that has historically been done by a man are all invested in toxic masculinity to some degree; some, such as the uniformed services, banking and finance, to an extraordinary degree. You can, however, adjust and adapt, though be careful how much you adjust and adapt as it means you end up colluding in that which oppresses you. I discuss this at length in Chapter 7.

Does it matter if I am a feminist woman and I want to employ a man who I think is a male Resister? Having had over 55 years in regular employment, most of that as a manager, leader, director or similar, my own yardstick is not to knowingly recruit or employ anyone who is racist, misogynistic or homophobic. While I fully support professional development in gender and race awareness, some individuals have such entrenched prejudices as to be beyond recovery, at least for the organisation. So better to weed these out at the recruitment stage rather than allow the toxicity to enter the lifeblood of the organisation.

As a woman, should I have zero tolerance towards men with toxic masculinity and who are Resisters? I think you should have zero tolerance towards anyone who abuses others in any way at all. That said, each situation will be different and you'll have to judge for yourself how you feel about it. But many men with toxic masculinity do have the potential to change for the better, so don't give up on them all. Cut men a little slack because it isn't easy leaving the 'bliss' of ignorance for the 'starkness' of enlightenment. Men will experience fear and anxiety. We are asking them to give up a way of being a man which they've never had to question before in their lives. Being in toxic masculinity, especially more extremes versions, is like being addicted to drugs, gambling or alcohol. If the man wants to change, recognises and accepts how their behaviour messes them up and everyone close to them, then, yes, definitely help them move forward. Most will be unable to do it on their own.

If I just want a guy for sex and not a relationship, does it matter if he is a Resister or not? If you can retain control over the encounter and not leave yourself physically or emotionally vulnerable, then I don't see a problem. In other words, you don't do anything you are not comfortable with. If you are always acting in consent and never pressured or under threat, then enjoy the sex for what it is. See more on this in Chapter 8.

Do all those men who are Resisters realise they are? No, absolutely not. Most will merely see themselves as 'ordinary guys' who respect women and treat them well. And this may be true for many men with toxic masculinity. The problem is that their masculine identity relies on that crucial power factor to get validation. They will only treat well those who do not threaten their masculinity and do not emasculate them. Some Resisters, especially those who are male fundamentalists, will recognise they are resisting women's empowerment and be quite 'happy' about that, i.e. the incel.

I am in a relationship with a Resister but we are very happy together. I know he is vulnerable in his masculinity, but that attracts me. Is there a problem with this? This is a very common scenario and so long as your guy does not behave towards you in ways which are threatening, bullying, abusive, violent or emotionally controlling, then you can probably have a long term, satisfying relationship. All men are vulnerable in their masculinity. The ones you should be worried about are those men who try to overcome that vulnerability by being sexist, misogynistic, homophobic and racist. In other words, behaving aggressively and violently.

Are Resisters simply white working-class males who have lost their role and power in this new globalised society? No. Many will be exactly like this category of male, but they are not the majority. Resisters come in every skin colour, every social class, every wealth category, every religion and can be found in every region of the world.

Collapsed Masculinity: The Retreater

Just as power is the key to understanding the Resister, so it is with the Retreater, the difference being that for these individuals it is a retreat from power, or at least an unwillingness to exercise it in traditional masculine ways. Whether Retreater is living alone in his bedroom, shutting out the world, or has found comfort and solace in dressing like a woman, wearing a bra, using make-up and behaving in a stereotypically feminine manner, the fundamental drive behind his behaviour is a rejection of traditional male identity; call it hegemonic, toxic or simply masculine. He doesn't want to be a military man, a salaryman, a playboy, an alpha male or very masculine at all. He certainly desires none of the masculine apparatus which constructed his father and his father before him. This leaves the Retreater in a rather unique and unusual position in modern society. For example, while we can see quite clearly what he is not, it is much less clear just what he is. Below are 15 questions raised by this emergent male identity, together with my answers.

To what extent is the Retreater going through a crisis of masculinity? These men are not in crisis with their masculinity. They may be in crisis with their families, their friends and the dominant gender role model society wishes to impose on them, but they are not in crisis with who they are as individuals. Any crisis comes from the moral panic which now envelops governments of countries such as those in China, South Korea and Japan, who increasingly fear this type of male.

Why would countries such as China, South Korea and Japan fear the Retreater? Quite simply because he is seen as effeminate and soft, the very antithesis of what authoritarian and competitively capitalistic countries demand from their menfolk; hardness, discipline, ambition and, yes, the capacity to be violent to order. In essence, the Retreater is seen to be a threat to the continuation of a functioning society, one which has historically relied on hegemonic (toxic) masculinity for leadership and direction.

Is the Retreater in any way male? Only in so much as he has a penis. Beyond that, he is not male at all, at least when one defines maleness as the polar opposite to femininity. Sociologically speaking, the Retreater is not a 'masculine subject', which I define as follows:

> 'A masculine subject is an individual who has, both knowingly and unknowingly, taken on the masculinist discourses which configure the social landscape in which he lives and operates, to the extent that he has become them. His sense of self, and his sense of his manliness, is wholly invested in these ways of being, these dominant narratives of how it is to be a man.'[89]

Having rejected dominant and traditional masculine codes, especially those around work, sex and aggression, the Retreater is no longer masculine in the way society has historically defined it.

Is the Retreater a confused male? Not all, but many will be, especially those who find it difficult to create a narrative around who they are and what they seek from life. Those Retreaters who have adopted feminoid characteristics are likely to be less confused because they do have a clear identity model to relate to and replicate. And from this model they can develop positive and constructive ways of being in the world, especially if they are surrounded by other feminoids and supportive women. The more confused Retreaters will be among those who have, literally, retreated from all social contact, i.e. become Soloists (hikikomori).

Will a Retreater be a threat to women? No, by definition they cannot be a threat to women, to LGBT+ people or to other men. Aggressiveness is not part of their emotional repertoire. They are passive, docile and do not acquire a sense of manliness by needing to exert control and power over others.

Can a Retreater make a good partner? The small percentage of feminoids who desire full relationships with women will make excellent partners as long as they are first able to overcome their reticence and engage with women, i.e. be forthcoming and open. Many feminoids appear unable to do this, and instead rely on women making the first move in any potential romantic encounter. Those Retreaters who have physically removed themselves from society will hardly be in a position to begin a relationship let alone maintain one.

If the number of Retreaters grows in the world, what are the implications for relationships? This is one of the scenarios I explore in the final chapter, but essentially the implications for relationships will be good in terms of how males and females relate to each other socially and in terms of a decline in male violence and competitiveness, but definitely not good in terms of population

[89]   Whitehead, S. M. (2002) *Men and Masculinities.* Cambridge: Polity. (see Chapter 7)

growth. In other words, more social harmony between the sexes, but a lot less sexual intimacy.

Will all Retreaters be feminists? Most will be, though bearing in mind that feminism comes in many different varieties, one can expect most Retreaters to be pro-LGBT+ and certainly unfazed by female power.

If I am a woman who is attracted to a Retreater, how do I go about starting a relationship? The only chance of a Retreater getting into any relationship is if he puts himself out there, which means making himself physically available to women. I've known Retreaters do this by finally plucking up the courage to go to a bar and meet women, Retreaters who have fallen in love with their Counsellor, and Retreaters who have gone online to meet women via dating apps. This latter option is the most common.

What should I know about a Retreater before I get into a relationship with one? If they have made the effort to meet women then the main driver behind that will be sex, in which case you need not be concerned that he doesn't want a sexual relationship. He will. The positives of being in a relationship with a Retreater are that he is unlikely to play around with other women, will not be aggressive, will be very willing and capable about revealing his feelings, will have high good emotional intelligence, and be loyal. On the negative side, just watch out for any Retreater who gets too attached and is unable to give you space.

Are Retreaters vulnerable men, like Resisters? We are all vulnerable to some extent. Any person who claims to be invulnerable is kidding you and themselves. The Retreater's sense of himself is not, however, reliant on performing as an alpha male and receiving constant validation that he is a 'man's man'. Retreater has rejected all that. He will certainly have gone through some self-analysis to get to be the person he is, and in rejecting masculinity he will have had to work out who and what he now is. Any Retreater who has got this far in their subjective journey is going to be as secure as anyone can be.

You have identified two sub-types within the genre of Collapsed Masculinity – are these not two different masculinities? Possibly, and perhaps another sociologist will develop such an analysis. However, for me the fact that neither type is actively seeking the replication of toxic masculinity, nor has moved onto progressive masculinity, shows that they occupy a third model of being which is essentially non-masculine. Given that masculinity is an edifice which constantly needs to be pumped up in order to survive, Retreater is definitely not contributing to that 'pumping up'. He is, therefore, contributing to the collapse of masculinity, though many Retreaters may not see it that way or be aware of it.

Are feminoids simply gay men or transgenders who are too afraid of coming out? It is entirely possible that a few will be, but not the majority. Gay masculinity has its own sub-types, and while one or two of these types may correspond with the feminoid, they are fundamentally defined around gay desire and sexual expression. That is not who the Retreater is. He is straight, very likely celibate, withdrawn or expressing himself in a stereotypically feminine way. Gay men do not reject masculinity; they create their own definitions of it. The Retreater is biologically male but socially rejecting TM.

Would the Retreater have come into existence without modern feminism? While the Retreater can be seen as one consequence of modern feminism, modern feminism has not created him. Feminism has not emasculated these men. Society has tried to masculinise them but failed. There is a big difference here. If you want to know more about the dynamics behind the emergence of feminoids and soloist/hikikimori males, look at the strident and unrelenting competitiveness of modern global capitalist society; the rigidity of gender and sex roles in Asia and elsewhere; the lack of opportunity for males to perform hegemonic masculine roles in a society where technology is changing not just how we earn money, but what we can be; the inherent aggressiveness of dominant masculinity; even the stress of educational achievement. All these and more have made young men question who they are and what they might be. Add in the ingredient of feminism and women's growing assertiveness, then the mix is complete. No single part is enough; all parts have needed to be in place to create the Retreater. Given that none of these parts appears to be going away, and are indeed in place worldwide, then it seems reasonable to assume that more men will become Retreaters.

Can Retreaters be 'cured' of their femininity and passivity? Well the Chinese authorities certainly hope so, which is why they are trying hard to make 'young boys more masculine'. More on this in my final chapter. But really it won't succeed. It is a classic example not just of moral panic among the conservatives in power, but also of older men trying to make younger men into carbon copies of themselves. Society is constantly changing and the Retreater gives some clues as to what direction it may go in.

Progressive Masculinity: The Embracer

'Equal opportunities' is a concept like birthdays; everyone gets to eat cake, even if it's only once a year. Unfortunately, as many men are now starting to realise, equal opportunities means a whole lot more than that. It means spreading the cake a lot thinner, leaving men, as a gender group, worse off as a consequence. There is only so much cake to go around and the more women in power and in employment, the fewer men. Add in the fact that worldwide, females are outperforming males across the educational spectrum, then equal opportunities will equal less opportunity for a lot of men. It comes as no surprise, therefore, to learn that *"from criminal justice to business to mental health, evidence suggests the position of women is not improving"*, with the World Economic Forum warning that *"movement towards gender parity was shifting into reverse"*.[90]

Is this slowdown towards gender parity deliberate or incidental? Are men in power actively firming up against equal opportunities or are they doing their best in the face of difficult economic and social pressures? One cannot answer for all men, but for sure the only men that women can expect to be on their side will be this man – the Embracer. Any other masculine type is unlikely to be standing up for women. Men with toxic masculinity will, at the very best, only pay lip service to women's rights, no more. They won't be active and truly supportive because they don't really believe in the cause. It is not their cause. As for the Retreater, many will be supportive, but this male type isn't interested in holding the reins of power anyway; they are not competing in the game so don't expect them to be the ones making big strategic policy decisions in organisations or in government.

The Embracer is more than a good guy to have on your side if you are a feminist; he is the only guy you will have on your side and who can actually help you.

Below are 12 questions about the Embracer, and my answers.

Are men born Embracers or do they learn this way of being a man? Both. There are many millennials who are Embracers and have progressive masculine identity, and they exist everywhere, not just in the West. Some will have become progressive through their upbringing and education, others (like myself) through exposure to feminism and feminists. No male is born with a masculinity; it can only be acquired through the social learning process – by osmosis mostly.

Will all Embracers be progressive in other aspects of their identity, e.g. anti-racism, environmental protection, human rights, democratic processes? Yes. While Embracers may have different political views, it is impossible for any man who is supportive of women's rights and is a pro-feminist to not be anti-racist and liberal in other areas of his life. One cannot pick and choose one's causes. One is either for openness and equality, or not.

Are Embracers always non-religious? No. Embracers exist in all religions and faiths, though they will not be religious radicals. In other words, they will not

---

[90] https://www.weforum.org/press/2017/11/ten-years-of-progress-on-global-gender-parity-stalls-in-2017

be highly conservative in their views. Many Embracers will be spiritual rather than religious, not following any particular religious dogma but at the same time being spiritually aware and open-minded.

How do I know if a man is an Embracer? Very easy: you ask him the question posed above in this chapter regarding the Declaration of Gender Rights, making sure he knows it includes LGBT+ people as well as straight women. If you know the guy well enough then you can check his practice against his answer.

What material benefits are there for a man who is an Embracer of women's rights and power? The material benefits are that he is likely to be more successful in work, especially if he is demonstrating emotional intelligence in his dealings with people. He is likely to acquire more cultural capital due to his ability to co-operate with diverse groups, and he exemplifies the growing need that complex organisations have for leaders and managers with empathy and self-awareness.

What emotional benefits are there for a man who is an Embracer of women's rights and power? The benefits include having more productive and stronger relationships with his loved ones, partner and any children. He will be able and willing to express himself and not get unduly defensive when challenged over his behaviour. He will be a communicator, not a retreater or an attacker in a relationship. Really the biggest single advantage these men have over men with toxic masculinity is their heightened self-awareness, their emotional intelligence and their capacity for empathy.

If I am in a relationship with an Embracer will he always be faithful? I discuss the sex issue in Chapter 8, where I stress that is important to understand masculinity and sexuality as distinct aspects of a man's identity. Although these identities do overlap, you cannot assume that a guy with progressive masculinity is going to be make a good husband, a faithful and considerate lover, or not have some vices. Some will, some won't. There are aspects of being a man which go beyond masculinity, and sexuality is one of the most important.

Is there any disadvantage to having an organisation only employing men with progressive masculinity, and none with toxic masculinity? Some men with toxic masculinity can be tolerated in large organisations, as long as is it not in the male leaders and managers. If it is, then the organisation has a big problem. In that case, it requires focused professional development to wean these men off their discriminatory responses: if they are leaders, they will resent and resist this. Also bear in mind that leaders and managers tend to 'recruit in their own image', so the most important job for any owner or CEO is to ensure that those who do the recruiting are progressives, not toxic in their attitude. This applies to both women and men leaders. As for having an organisation full of men with progressive masculinity, as long as they are recruited on merit, including emotional intelligence, then the organisation will be much stronger for it.

Can a Resister become an Embracer? Yes, as long as he has not succumbed to male fundamentalism. If he has, then changing him will require mental health intervention; it cannot be done by his partner or family alone. This is discussed at length in Chapters 8 and 9, but be aware that changing many men from being Resisters to being Embracers can often require them to be undone from any strident religious ideology. So, for a lot of guys, you are asking them to become someone else – you are asking them to change some core aspects of their identity and most won't have the desire, strength or confidence to do this, especially if they perceive this as their having to become 'less manly', less 'powerful' in order to embrace feminism and women's rights. It is just too big a leap for them.

Is it impossible for an Embracer to be aggressive and violent? It is quite possible. If pushed, most anyone – man or woman – can be violent, if only in defence of themselves or their loved ones. But with the Embracer, violence, abuse and aggression are not habitualised in him. This doesn't make every Embracer passive and totally non-violent; it just means he is better able to control his emotions and emotional responses.

If I am a man concerned that I may have toxic masculinity, how do I change to become an Embracer? This is discussed in Chapter 10 but frankly, if you are sincere in your desire to change and self-aware enough to ask this question in the first place, then you are more than halfway there. Just put down any defensiveness you may be feeling and recognise what this will mean for you and yours if you can become a man in tune with the 21st century, not one living in a Victorian, or worse, medieval, mindset.

I have read articles and seen YouTube videos of men who claim that what women really want is an alpha male, a guy who will protect them, take control and be dominant. What do you think? If you've managed to read this far in the book, then you already know what I think. Carry on reading.

Part Three

Women, Sexuality

Chapter Seven

Women and Toxic Masculinity

Woman has always been subordinate to man. Women have internalised the alien point of view that man is the essential, woman the inessential.[91]

The purpose of this book is not to interrogate women's relationship to toxic masculinity, but at the same time, to ignore this relationship is to remain only partially aware both of the deep rootedness of this masculinity and the ways it gets normalised.

There can be little doubt that one of the single biggest reasons why toxic masculinity has become the default masculinity for most males is because women have allowed it. Too many women have been prepared to accommodate toxic masculine behaviour as the standard of maleness, even when in so doing they suffered as a consequence. More than this, many women actively participate in the continuation of toxic masculinity. Women must face up to their complicity in this. Until they do so, the problem will continue.

For the 30 years that I've been studying and researching this topic I've been continuously reminded of one fact: women can be ardent apologists for men.

Why We Should All Be Feminists

A 2016 survey by the Fawcett Society revealed that only 7% of Britons consider themselves to be feminists.[92] This mirrors my experience of asking women if they are feminists. Most will say "no", some will say "not sure" and a few will say "yes". But whatever their response, the vast majority will be keen to let you know that for them, being a feminist is "not about oppressing men".

This desire to not be seen as "oppressors of men" is, frankly, staggering to me as a man. It tells me that women continue to put the feelings of men first; not their own rights, needs, or indeed, safety. For centuries, 50% of the population has been active in the oppression and marginalisation of the other

---

[91] McCall, D. K. 'Simone de Beauvoir, *The Second Sex,* and Jean-Paul Sartre', in *Signs: Journal of Women in Culture and Society.* 5, No2, p. 210.

[92] https://www.fawcettsociety.org.uk/News/we-are-a-nation-of-hidden-feminists

50%. Actually, it is more like 40% doing the oppressing if you allow for the LGBT+ ratio to be included. This could not happen in any other geopolitical domain.

When the white South Africans were rightly called out over their racism towards Black Africans, the world, pretty much as a whole, stood with the accusers and not with the accused. Everyone was keen to get on the anti-apartheid platform. No such global voice speaks for women, not even today. Women are forced to defend themselves against every conceivable form of discrimination, violence and oppression, much of it institutionalised and grounded in religious dogma. And yet still few men stand up alongside them. If women do not shout and resist, and do so loudly, few men will shout for them – that much is clear.

Yes, one can blame the masculinist media for much of this – their desire to not upset men in power, to maintain the gender status quo, and to go for the easy option which has been to discredit any woman angry and confident enough to stand up and say "men have a problem' or men "are oppressors of women". But now women too own and contribute to the media. They too can use social media to express their opinions. Which makes it remarkable that even today, three years after MeToo, and after centuries of male power, large numbers of women still want to maintain the myth that love and caring will get men with toxic masculinity to change.

'Call out culture' has become a problematic mentality where the act of calling out becomes more important than conversing. This defeats the point. Without deconstructing problematic actions, ideas, and habits, we end up with a situation where both parties feel threatened, and act out aggressively. Making sure your intention is constructive is important, because if you didn't care enough about that person, or about continuing your relationship, you wouldn't be explaining why their actions or words are hurtful or against your ethics.[93]

This quote is from an article published in *Marie Claire* in December 2018. The piece is designed to help 'Modern Man' redefine his masculinity. It hopes to do this by women "talking about toxic masculinity with the men in your life." The short article encapsulates the problem that many women have with men's toxic masculine behaviour. They don't want to seriously confront it. They hope by adopting the stance of an amateur relationship therapist – listening, being considerate, remaining patient and especially doing and saying nothing that might in any way be interpreted by their male partner as threatening or confrontational – they will be able to get their man to change his attitude and behaviour.

---

[93]   http://www.marieclaire.co.za/hot-topics/unlearn-toxic-masculinity-modern-man

This is at best a naïve hope, and at worst only strengthens a man's belief that he can carry on as he has been doing, and as his male ancestors did, without any real challenge to his toxic masculinity. Very few men will willingly divest themselves of the toxic masculine cloak they've got around them. It requires too much self-analysis, is too threatening and too much of a risk to his ingrained sense of himself as a man. Talking nicely to him is not going to work. Men must be confronted with the consequences of their masculine assumptions. Men must go through the detoxification stages I identify in Chapter 10. No one should assume this will be easy.

One has to recognise the elephant in the room here, which is that straight women desire men, and many of the men they desire as lovers, partners or husbands are in truth unsuitable and in many instances dangerous. This does suggest that a great many women are prepared to forgo respect in exchange for having a man in their life, at least one who professes to love them. There can be no other reasonable explanation for the fact that women, even in the 21st century, can compartmentalise or ignore the violences done to their sisters and to themselves, and yet remain at the very least ambivalent feminists, and in many cases, anti-feminist. It is, indeed, the equivalent of the oppressed supporting their oppressors.

Of course, there are exceptions, instances where women have suffered so much at the hands of men that they've been forced to take direct action to protect themselves from the men in their midst.

During the 1980s, two women anthropologists from Australia studied several remote 'stone age' tribes in the jungles of New Guinea. The scientists discovered two tribes that had appeared to have resolved the incessant fighting between men in these tribes and between men of different tribes. The women, wives, had got so fed up with the violence and the fact that their sons invariably became caught up in it that they decided, as a group of women, to take action in the only way they could. They culled the male babies. In effect, they reduced the number of male children in the tribes by killing many of them at birth. This created what became, as a consequence, a matriarchal tribal society. The number of violent males reduced, the whole culture of violence in the tribes was eventually eradicated. Peace ensued.[94]

It is November 2018, and at the end of a long dusty road in the plains of northern Syria, a young woman with a rifle over her shoulder guards the entrance to the isolated village of Jinwar. This hamlet is a women-only commune for Kurdish women to escape the family-orientated roles that a patriarchal society had assigned to them. "There is no place for men here, our lives are good," says Zainab, a 28-year-old resident. "This place is just for women who want to stand

[94] https://able2know.org/topic/126311-1 and https://www.brisbanetimes.com.au/world/png-highland-women-kill-male-babies-20081201-geam13.html

on their own two feet... Without women there is no freedom. Until women educate and empower themselves, there won't be freedom."[95]

It is worth reflecting just how much women are prepared to tolerate before they say "enough"; before they take extreme action and decide to retreat to their women-only communes, or reduce the number of males in their society.

I am sure that if the roles had been reversed, and men had been born into a matriarchal society that marginalised and discriminated against them in every conceivable way, and in numerous instances enslaved, abused and murdered them, that they'd be up in arms pretty fast. Already, today, we can hear men shouting "unfair" and worse at women who are confronting them with their behaviours. I've personally had numerous men call me out on my attitude to male violence and my feminist stance, demanding I give more attention to the "numerous instances of women being violent towards men".

Men can be very quick to adopt the label of 'victim' when it comes to women's behaviour towards them, which is in stark contrast to the historic and remarkable forbearance shown by women towards the violence done to them by men, often men who are their 'loved ones'.

When I've talked to some women about their reluctance to adopt the label 'feminist', I've often heard the comment; "well, women do need protecting and it is good to have a man to do that for you." I have to ask them, "what do you need protecting from?" And the answer, inevitably, is men. Women co-opt men to protect them from other men. And in so doing they immediately forego their feminine independence; their inalienable right to live in peace and free from male aggression and dominance.

The fear that stalks a woman walking the streets alone at night is not fear of a female murderer or rapist, it is fear of the male. This is what toxic masculinity engenders. It is a way of being a man that doesn't need to be acted out in daily life to be powerful. Its toxicity is ever-present in our imaginations and our darkest fears.

A Sisterhood?

Every time I hear a woman tell me she is not a feminist, I quietly despair. Accepting she is entitled to her opinion, and indeed may well have bought into the media-inspired ridiculous stereotypes surrounding feminists and feminism, the reality is that she is denying the existence of a sisterhood and therefore undermining the efforts of women to achieve, at the very least, parity with men, and hopefully full freedom from patriarchal conditions globally. Yes, I know, 'sisterhood' is a dated concept with women and even with many feminists,

[95] https://app.independent.co.uk/2018/12/02/welcome-to-jinwar-a-women-only-village-in-syria-that-wants-to-smash-the-patriarchy/content.html

but without some sense of a sisterhood – a unifying and unified approach by women to changing the gender status quo – the battle will be much harder. Women cannot fully rely on the minority of men who are progressives. There are just not enough of them. In many countries they are a tiny minority. Women can only bring about change themselves. Men won't do it for them.

Women should be under no illusions about this because for sure, most men believe in the male equivalent of a sisterhood: a brotherhood; a unifying sense of being blokes together against the rest. This ideology lurks everywhere men gather in groups and it always excludes women. In fact a key element of the male bonding process is the exclusion of women.

One would hope and expect that educated, middle class women, especially those in positions of power, influence and authority would lead on this. And indeed, many do. Examples that come to mind are Emma Watson, Angelina Jolie and Viola Davis. But I've come across many women who have no desire to stand up for gender justice. They adopt the 'Margaret Thatcher stance': *'I appoint people only on merit, not on gender. If they are good enough, then I don't care what gender they are'*. That would be all very well if it weren't for the fact that women need to prove themselves not only equal to men, but better than men. Women start from a position of having to compromise their femininity in order to progress up the masculinist career ladder. They have to become adept at impression management; they have to learn to give the impression that they are 'one of the lads, can cut it like the men, are as tough as the guys'. Margaret Thatcher was the iconic example of this, but most organisations will have one if not several.

Are these women blinded to feminism or are they frightened of it? Do they see it as a toxic label with which they don't want to be associated, or do they genuinely think that it is all about taking people on 'their merit' and that this alone will remove centuries of sexism? Perhaps they believe we truly are in a post-feminist era, their success at climbing the ladder merely being evidence of this fact?

Or are these women being more strategic, deliberately attempting to manage their identity performance in a world which remains inherently masculinist?

The feminist sociologist, Sylvia Gherardi, has described this attempt by women to manage their impression to fit the prevailing masculinist organisational culture as 'schizogenic'.[96] They are constantly attempting to straddle two gender identities – the masculine and the feminine. The woman is judged both as a woman and as leader, manager, professional, etc. The man is judged only in his work role, not by his gender. Women may not theorise their experiences in this way, but they certainly know they are doing it. They know

---

[96]   Gherardi, S. (1995) *Gender, Symbolism and Organizational Cultures*. London: Sage.

when they are engaging in gendered impression management. It is consciously done. Every day of their lives.

> As I moved up the management ladder I learned to wear certain types of outfits, dark colours, like a man's suit, still feminine but not girly, girly. I eventually stopped carrying a handbag to work and replaced it with a briefcase. Just like my male colleagues did. I learned to be more assertive, even aggressive sometimes in meetings. It wasn't who I was when I started out. But it is the woman I became, at least when I was working. But it really didn't matter what I did, I was always seen first as a woman, and second as a leader. I knew a lot of the decisions were made in the men's loo. (Jane, UK college manager)

Most men do not have the faintest idea this dilemma even exists for women. It is completely beyond their understanding. They lack the knowledge. They have absolutely no insight beyond the limited realm of masculine subjectivity that they inhabit.

In an age of globalised information, when self-reflectivity and self-knowledge are becoming increasingly important, and indeed provide the source for the 'cultural capital' from which we can develop as individuals in the world, men are becoming supremely disadvantaged by being men. They have never, at least until very recently, had to critically consider what it means to be a man. Now they are having to face searching questions about themselves, about their attitudes towards women and about their gender. They are only now starting to face the issues inherent in their masculine sense of self. This will be a long slow road, resisted by many men and aided by only a minority.

In the mid-1990s an intense intellectual discussion opened up within Western feminist academia. It concerned to what extent there was, or could be, a 'feminine/female knowledge'.[97] That is, a way of thinking and being in the world which was exclusive to women/females and largely outside the comprehension of straight males especially. This enforced the idea that women were a distinct community based on their experiences of the world. The discussion ebbed and flowed between the various feminist theoretical camps, but ultimately the argument was made that if you are born a female then the very fact of that gender labelling from birth means you are going to be experiencing the world as a female. Having the male gaze constantly upon you shapes a woman's sense of herself and gives women particular experiences, knowledges and insights denied to men. Women's epistemological relationship to the world is filtered through that experience and it is unique to females. This gives her a unique knowledge foundation from which to receive, engage in and understand the world.

---

[97] See Whitehead, S. M. (2002) *Men and Masculinities.* Cambridge: Polity. Chapter 2.

Dustin Hoffman's experience of playing a woman in Sydney Pollack's film *Tootsie* confronted him with this awareness and he found it to be traumatic.

> *If I was going to be a woman, I would want to be as beautiful as possible. And they [the producers] said to me 'Uh, that's as beautiful as we can get you.' And I went home and started crying to my wife, and I said 'I have to make this picture,' and she said, 'Why?' And I said, 'Because I think I am an interesting woman when I look at myself on screen, and I know that if I met myself at a party, I would never talk to that character because she doesn't fulfil, physically, the demands that we're brought up to think that women have to have in order for us to ask them out.' She says, 'What are you saying?' and I said, 'There's too many interesting women I have not had the experience to know in this life because I have been brainwashed."* It was not what I felt like to be a woman. It was what it felt like to be someone that people didn't respect, for the wrong reasons. I know it's a comedy but it was not a comedy for me. For me it was a serious business.[98]

The everyday sexism and misogyny that women experience is not experienced by men. Something similar will be experienced by many gay men but gay men do have the option of masking themselves up as straight guys, and many do, precisely in order to avoid negative judgement, discrimination or worse. Women have no such option. And this experience is both enlightening and, as Hoffman came to realise, potentially very painful at least in a world where men have ruled.

In effect, what the feminist theorists were arguing in regard to a 'female epistemology/community' was made explicit by Hoffman's experience of portraying himself as a woman on screen. For Hoffman, a man, it was nothing less than an epiphany. For women it is their everyday life. They know what it is like to live with this constant knowledge of having to manage oneself in a way which is deemed socially acceptable for a female/woman. Men do not have this knowledge. And it disadvantages them.

It is more than a cliché to state that 'women know men better than men know themselves'. It is patently true, because women's knowledge of the world is so much broader, so much more developed, so much more insightful and so much more accurate.

If you have any doubts about that statement, just do a simple test:

Ask any straight man the following question:

> *How has being a man affected your experience of work/family/life?* (delete as you feel necessary)

---

[98]   https://www.huffingtonpost.in/2013/07/08/dustin-hoffman-brainwashed-about-female-beauty_n_3561585.html

And ask any woman this question:

How has being a woman affected your experience of work, of family, of life?

See what the responses are and to what extent they are different. At the very least you are likely to find that most women are able to answer the question.

Accepting that every woman is her own person, an individual with her own unique life, history and identity, the fact of her being a woman places her on one side of the gender binary whether she chooses to be there or not. This is a unifying position because it is a position held by all women regardless of their race, sex, class, religion or nationality. She, like all women, is the 'Other' not by choice, not by biology, but by male intent.

Women's internalisation of their own 'otherness' is manifested in the comments of those women who deny feminism, who deny the possibility of a sisterhood, and therefore continue to pay homage to the toxic masculinity which has historically tried to render them powerless.

Women are the Other not because they lack penises, but because they lack power.[99]

Why Do Some Women Participate in TM?

Historians suggest that FGM has been with us for at least 2,000 years, while the World Health Organization estimates that even today there are eight countries where FGM (female genital mutilation) is 80% prevalent.[100] This is about women cutting women and it is worth asking 'why?'. When a woman takes a knife and performs genital mutilation on a young girl, why is she doing that? Why is she performing the role of torturer of other females? There can only be two answers to that question.

1. She believes she is acting correctly as a woman, fulfilling a social, cultural and/or religious responsibility that all her womenfolk, down the centuries have adhered to.
2. She is afraid not to.

The first answer suggests she is a 'cultural dope'; that is, she is unable to see the conditions of her own oppression. The term 'cultural dope' comes from sociology[101] and is often used to explain the workings of ideology on the minds of individuals. For the woman performing FGM, this is what is means to be

[99] Simone de Beauvoir, quoted in R. Tong (1994) *Feminist Thought*. London: Routledge. Chapter 7.

[100] https://www.who.int/reproductivehealth/topics/fgm/prevalence/en

[101] See, for discussion, Lynch, M. (2012) 'Revisiting the Cultural Dope', in *Human Studies*, 35(2).

a woman. She doesn't see FGM as you and I see it, an horrific, life-changing violation of the human rights of girls and women. Nor does she see herself as a willing accomplice in the ongoing oppression of females. She is simply obeying the codes and expectations of her culture.

In reality, whether she is doing this act for the first reason or the second, she is of course obeying the rules of the men who control her society. She is a cultural dope to the ideology of patriarchy: male power.

FGM is just one example of how being a woman can lead to the continued oppression of other women. Here is another.

It was a chance for Lina (16) to leave her isolated village in one of the poorest parts of Indonesia, for neighbouring Malaysia, where some migrant workers can earn more in a few years than a lifetime at home. And in 2013, when migrant recruiter Sarah arrived in the village, offering to give Lina such a chance, she took it despite the reservations of her family. Sarah insisted they could trust her; she was related to the village chief. Still, Lina's family wanted to hold a Catholic prayer service for Lina before she left. Sarah promised she would only take Lina to the provincial capital of Kupang for one night to organise her paperwork, then bring her back the next day. It was a lie. Lina never came home, alive. Two years later, Lina's body was returned to her village. She had been beaten to death by her Malaysian female employer. Officials found bruises on Lina's head and face and infected wounds on her hands and legs. As a domestic slave in Malaysia, Lina had endured two years of torture.

Sarah deliberately used her femininity to create trust between herself and Lina's family, backed up by her relationship to the village chief. All the while, however, she was participating in the enforcement of toxic masculinity, because behind the scenes is a masculinist culture of female oppression, violence and death. It is commonplace in South East Asia, with tens of thousands of impoverished women driven into prostitution, slavery, sex trafficking and domestic abuse each year. Thousands of young women, like Lina, go home in a body bag.

But toxic masculinity doesn't have to be physically threatening to a woman for it to end up diminishing a woman's life:

Kalong (17) got pregnant with her boyfriend 18 months ago. They met through Facebook before having unprotected sex. Kalong's parents were horrified and insisted she have an abortion. Kalong cried and begged to be allowed to keep the baby; eventually they agreed. Kalong's boyfriend refused to take any responsibility for the child and now has no contact with her. Kalong's family are very poor. They are reliant on the 600 baht ($18) a month child allowance given to them by the Thai state. With the addition of Kalong's baby, the family now have seven grandchildren to be taken care of. The others were born to three unemployed daughters. Each daughter left their children with their parents.

Kalong and her family won't see themselves as victims of male power or toxic masculinity, but they are. Kalong's feckless absent father; the feckless absent fathers of the other three grandchildren; the wretched poverty that grinds young women into a situation where they appear to have no choice but to leave home and leave their children with their mother. The matriarch, aged 57, now having to cope with yet another baby.

I could fill this book with examples but no doubt you'll have your own. The point is that we stop seeing that which is obvious, either because we are ignorant of the reality, or we prefer not to look.

What happened two years ago, with MeToo, is that it opened women's eyes. And once a person sees differently, they cannot go back to unseeing. Once a person knows a truth, they cannot ever again unknow it. None of us today, women or men, can honestly claim to be ignorant of the reality.

But truths are dangerous. The reason why it took so long for feminism to get this far as a mainstream discourse is not simply because men tried to undermine it, but because women didn't want to hear it.

Many still don't want to hear it.

Because to hear it and accept it means having to renegotiate oneself as a woman in relation to men. It means looking at men in a different light, through a different gaze. Not a gaze of admiration and respect, desire and worship, but a gaze of scrutiny, mistrust and doubt.

How do I know this, as a man?

For the simple reason that men who engage with feminism have to do the same. They must go through a learning process which disengages them from the thoughts, ideas and actions inherent in toxic masculinity. This is not easy to do. Our attachment to dominant masculinity and to the gender binary and all it entails, is both existential and ontological: it is intense and deeply personal.

Men with toxic masculinity are so not because this is what women want from them, but because this way of being validates them with other men.

For much of history, what it meant to be a woman was to be the woman that men wanted you to be.

Even today, men remain the definers of the gender binary, not women. It is breaking out of that way of thinking, ceasing to accept men as the arbiters of what is 'normal', what is 'natural', that is so challenging. But so very necessary.

The Identity Trick

Are all women therefore collaborating with men in their own discrimination and oppression? Of course not. Feminism is now out and loud and global. It has become an immensely powerful discourse and many millions of women are active in promoting gender justice and challenging patriarchal conditions wherever they find them. However, equal opportunities for women and LGBT+ people, and all that entails, remains a distant dream. Only five countries (Britain, Bolivia, Ecuador, Fiji and Malta) have given constitutional rights to people regardless of their sexual orientation and gender identity.[102]

We can expect straight men to resist these changes. They have much to lose in terms of power and gender status once full constitutional rights are given to women and LGBT+ people. But that alone doesn't explain why so many women, too, resist being liberated from the conditions which render them less powerful than men; indeed, they participate in the continuing oppression of women by men.

One explanation brings us once again back to Simone de Beauvoir's notion of the 'Other'.

The reason why the woman wields the FGM knife; why the female migrant recruiter lies to another woman in order to profit from her enslavement; and why Kalong and her family are destined to a life of poverty, is because they do not view themselves as having value. As women, they must, under the rules of the patriarchal gender binary, enslave themselves. Men don't need to do it to them, women do it for themselves. They do it by accepting the notion that femininity is sacrifice, that to be a woman is to always be beholden to someone else; family, father, husband, lover or child.

> *The enslavement of the female to the species and the limitations of her various powers are extremely important facts... Biology is not enough to answer the question that is before us: why is woman the Other?... It is not in giving life but in risking life that man is raised above the animal: that is why superiority has been accorded to humanity not to the sex that brings forth but to that which kills.*[103]

And any woman who sees herself as having little value as a woman is likely to see other women in the same way.

To understand why toxic masculinity exists, and why it will be immensely difficult to eradicate, one must see and understand the identity trick at work here.

This is not simply about getting men to open up, acquire a little more reflexivity, stop abusing their partners and become kinder. It is about changing men fundamentally from what they are into something else; no longer men who see themselves as the centre, but men who no longer recognise a centre. To do that, women must first stop acceding to the codes of femininity that

---

[102] Raub, A, Cassola, A, Latz, I, Heymann, J. (2016) 'Protections of Equal Rights Across Sexual Orientation and Gender Identity: An Analysis of 193 National Constitutions' in Yale Journal of Law and Feminism, Vol. 28: 149.

[103] De Beauvoir, S. *The Second Sex.* p. 41.

have been written for them by men down the centuries. And the key code of femininity that most women continue to adopt is one of acquiescence to male power. Being and becoming a woman, even today, means adopting an identity that does not call out men for their behaviour, even when that behaviour directly threatens her.

Has this historical gendered response been reversed with MeToo? Have the last two years shown us the future? I am not sure. It may be an historical blip, a mere bump along the everlasting road of male power and women's 'otherness'. Or it may not. This question is revisited in the final chapter.

But if it is to become more than a blip, more than a mere inconvenience to men, then the dynamic must come from all women, especially women in power. And all women must recognise that they are politically aligned with LGBT+ people in this. Every homophobic straight woman is aligning herself with toxic masculinity. Every racist woman is aligning herself with toxic masculinity. Why? Because she is repeating the narrative of discrimination, hatred, intolerance and abuse that empowers toxic masculinity, thereby rendering her own marginalisation as a woman more inevitable. She should be under no illusion that the aggressive narrative will eventually get turned towards her.

When it comes to hatred, toxic masculinity does not discriminate; it is prejudiced towards anyone who is deemed to be the 'Other'.

Women can be sure only of other women as allies in this battle: men with toxic masculinity will recognise they have too much to lose, at least in terms of power over women and LGBT people. Men with collapsed masculinity may well be collaborators, but in many ways they merely reinforce femininity as 'otherness', which leaves the male progressives, the Embracers, as the hope for future change.

However, femininity and masculinity are not only defined by power. They are defined, at least in the mind of the individual, by something even more complex: sexuality.

Chapter Eight

Sexuality and Toxic Masculinity

There is no simple definition of sexuality, or explanation of its undoubted power. Sexuality as a concept... refers to the bundle of social phenomena that shape erotic life: laws, religion, domestic arrangements, diseases, violence and love – everything we evoke when we speak of the sexuality of a culture. And it refers to the level of the individual – to the pleasures and pains that can shape our lives for good or ill. Which is why our culture can't quite let it [sexuality] go. It still fuels the personal and social imagination.[104]

The two key points to keep in mind about the above quote are: 1. We don't fully understand sexuality and 2. It has a powerful control over us. It fuels society. Without it, society and humanity would cease to exist. And while this may well happen in the future (see Chapter 11), we are not quite there yet.

But before I go further, I should declare an interest in this particular topic.

Reflections on a Journey

At the beginning of 2018 I became voluntarily celibate, or asexual. I won't go into the precise circumstances, only to say that for the previous 25 years I'd been the very opposite of asexual. Some will have labelled me promiscuous, others would describe me as a man with a high libido combined with opportunity. Whatever, from the age of 14 sexuality was an integral part of my masculine identity. That said, by the time I reached 40, I'd only had sex with three women and two of those I'd married. So not exactly jumping from bed to bed, at least for my first 40 years. However, that was soon to change and the number of women I was having sex with grew rapidly from the age of 45. In fact, the number grew so much and so rapidly over the ensuing 20 years or more that eventually the interest wore off – the whole process had become predictable and repetitive. By the middle of 2016, aged 67, I'd slowed down considerably and 18 months later switched off altogether. By the time my libido did start to weaken I thought

[104] Seidman, S., Fischer, N. and Meeks, C. (Eds) (2011) *Introducing the New Sexuality Studies.* New York: Routledge.

I knew all there was to know about sex and sexuality, having done pretty much everything a consenting adult can do with other consenting adults. But I was wrong. I was totally unprepared for the peace and quiet that was to envelop my life once the 'sex monkey' finally got off my back. On reflection, I can see how sexuality controlled much of my behaviour throughout my adult life. And even while I was a relative late starter, not losing my virginity until the age of 18 and then being faithful through two marriages for the next 25 or more years, I was always in thrall to sex. I now look at society, and men and women, in a different light, certainly as far as sexuality is concerned. I can see that no one is in control of their sexuality, at least not 100% in control. And most of us are its slaves; it determines our present and predicts our futures much more than we'd like to admit. And this situation is definitely more about biology than society.

My own research and personal experience support the numerous studies which show that sexuality is a given. It is not genetic, not a consequence of our DNA, but is biologically, not socially determined, likely through the interaction of testosterone in the womb.[105] We cannot change where we are positioned on the sexual continuum. I have tried, and I know many men and women who have tried also, but in the end as far as sexual identity is concerned, we are what they are born as: straight, gay or bi. This doesn't mean that straight men cannot have sex with other straight men or with gay men. They might well; it just depends on the social circumstances in which they are located. But two straight men having sex together does not make them gay. They are still straight. Likewise, with women and same-sex relationships.

This is important to understand in respect of toxic masculinity, because while a male can be weaned off toxic masculine behaviour, his sexuality remains predictable and immutable.

So does this mean that men with toxic masculinity are going to have a particular form of straight sexuality?

Yes and no. Toxic masculinity will not make a gay man straight, a straight man gay, or a bi man neither. But toxic masculinity will influence how a man internalises and expresses his sexuality. Importantly, while not defining a man's sexuality, toxic masculinity is more likely to make the expression of that sexuality problematic for the man and for those he connects with, both sexually and socially.

In other words, toxic masculine behaviour will to some extent also render a man's sexuality toxic.

At this point a question should be raised about the apparent contradiction in the above sentences. That is, if sexuality is biological then how can a social dynamic (masculinity) affect it?

[105] https://www.sciencemag.org/news/2012/12/homosexuality-may-start-womb

The answer lies in this statement:

Sex is who we go to bed with, gender is who we go to bed as.

Being straight is an indicator of desire, not an indicator of how that desire is going to get played out or exercised either in society or in the bedroom. To understand the practice, we need to look at the politics.

Political Sex Acts

Below are four contemporary male sexuality scenarios. While being different, taken together they illustrate some of the issues that surface when a culture obsessed with sexuality is framed around toxic masculinity and its masculinist value system.

Writer and former model, Stina Sanders (26) says she receives two or three sexual images from men each day. She has done so for the past three to five years and says all are unwanted. "When I first started receiving them it was truly shocking and awful. I don't want to see that," she said. "I'm actually quite used to it now, desensitised to it." Sometimes, she said, she has messaged the men back – asking why they were doing this. "A lot of people don't respond, but a lot people say they just want to say hello". "So say hello! There are lots of ways to do that."[106]

Kim (24) lives in Seoul. Last year she moved out of her family home to gain independence and be nearer her job. "I made sure it was a safe and secure place that I moved to. A lot of friends warned me against finding a place lower than five storeys because you could be targeted. I deliberately chose the 22nd Floor." Unfortunately, height didn't save her. One evening a policeman showed up at her front door with a high-end camera in hand. He informed Kim a man had been caught filming her from a rooftop of a six-floor building a distance of over 300 metres away. Kim is just one of the millions of South Korean women who have been victims of the 'secret camera' phenomena, with women being secretly filmed in washrooms, subways, classrooms and hotel rooms.[107]

Guida (14) lives in the North Eastern Indian state of Bihar. In October 2018 she and 35 of her female schoolfriends were hospitalised after being attacked by a large crowd of teenage boys and their parents, after complaining of sexual harassment. The girls had been playing in a sports area one Saturday night when a group of teenage boys began making lewd comments. The girls argued back and some physically remonstrated with the boys, who initially backed off. However, they returned later with some of their parents carrying bamboo sticks and iron rods. "They dragged us by our ponytails, assaulted us

[106] https://www.bbc.com/news/uk-46280798

[107] https://www.npr.org/2018/10/19/648720360/south-korean-women-fight-back-against-spy-cams-in-public-bathrooms

with bamboo sticks and kicked and punched us. We were totally unarmed and had nothing to protect us. I saw many of my friends lying on the ground and crying with pain. The girls admitted to hospital were aged between 10 and 14. Guida said the young men were angry "because we had protested against their sexual advances."[108]

Mike (50) is a marketing director for a London company. He is gregarious and sociable. His preferred style of communication, both with colleagues and friends, is to be tactile. So a lot of touching, double-hand shaking, friendly 'punching', hugs, sometimes a peck on the cheek. He also likes to tell jokes and smutty ones are his preference. Four months ago, a female colleague complained that Mike was harassing her and that his behaviour was inappropriate. The complaint was made after Mike told a particularly sexually explicit joke in her presence and later asked her out for dinner. Mike is currently under suspension while his case is being reviewed.

'Dick pics', as they are often described, are becoming 'normal' especially for a generation raised on Instagram, Facebook, Twitter and 'sexting', with young women becoming 'desensitised' to it. The invasion of women's privacy through the use of secret cameras, especially in South Korea but increasingly globally, has been one of the spurs behind the rise of MeToo and activist feminism in South Korea; the 'anti-molka' movement sweeping the nation since May 2018. India clearly has a problem with toxic masculinity and was recently declared the world's most dangerous country for women, while in many countries, especially America, men are assessing the risks they take when they associate with female colleagues:

No more dinners with female colleagues. Don't sit next to them on flights. Book hotel rooms on different floors. Avoid one-to-one meetings. A manager in infrastructure investing said he won't meet with female employees in rooms without windows anymore. He also keeps his distance in elevators. A late-40 something in private equity said he has a new rule, established on the advice of his wife, an attorney: no business dinner with a woman 35 or younger. The changes can be subtle but insidious, with a woman, say, excluded from casual after-work drinks, leaving male colleagues to bond, or having what should be a private meeting with a boss with the door left wide open.[109]

It seems that many men are now increasingly finding it hard to strike a balance between the sexual harassment of women and no contact with women whatsoever.

[108] https://www.theguardian.com/world/2018/oct/08/indian-schoolgirls-beaten-for-resisting-boys-sexual-advances

[109] https://www.bloomberg.com/news/articles/2018-12-03/a-wall-street-rule-for-the-metoo-era-avoid-women-at-all-cost

What is going on here with men?

The practices identified above are not driven by biology but by the social conditioning which men have experienced as they aged. Such discourses, as ways of expressing one's sexuality, become habitualised and engrained in the thinking of men and of women. They are most definitely not gender neutral; they are not benign. They range from the bizarrely obscene to the violent, their commonality being that they are all outcomes of toxic masculinity. Even the fact of men pulling away from female colleagues so as to avoid the risk of being accused of inappropriate behaviour only has one outcome and it is not to negate toxic masculinity either in the man or in the organisation. On the contrary, it serves to push women and men even further apart. It increases women's marginalisation in an organisation and is a complete failure of the organisation to recognise and address the gender dynamics at work here. And at that point, toxic masculinity is no longer being diminished; it has returned to normalisation, leaving the masculinist work culture untouched.

Sexuality as Destiny

Sexuality certainly influences our destiny, but what exactly that destiny might end up being depends to a great extent on the culture one is born into and lives in. If the culture is heavily invested in toxic masculinity, patriarchal values and sexism/misogyny, then whether it be a Wall Street bank and the Houses of Parliament, or India and South Korea, women are at risk, as are LGBT+ people. Indeed, how LGBT + people are treated by a society is the bellwether for how women will be treated. No society can make progress with women's rights and the negation of toxic masculinity, while still remaining prejudiced towards LGBT+ people, which makes it especially frustrating for me whenever I have talked to women who are avidly homophobic or, as is the case with many, still treating gay identity as a mental aberration or a 'sin'.

On the plus side, global research clearly shows that homosexuality is gathering greater acceptance and tolerance, even in those countries where same-sex relationships have long been sanctioned under law and religious diktat. The number of countries legalising same sex marriage increases each year, and at time of writing has reached thirty; up from one (Netherlands) in 2000.[110] The Philippines and Vietnam are both working towards a similar law, while Thailand is set to legalise civil partnerships which could grant gay couples the same rights as heterosexual ones. In tandem with a liberalisation of gender and sexual attitudes, in September 2017 Canada became the 10th country to offer its citizens gender-neutral passports, while in August 2019, Kenya became

---

[110] www.goodmorningamerica.com/culture/story/30-countries-sex-marriage-officially-legal-56041136

the first African country to include intersex people in their national population census, an important step forward for LGBT+ rights in Africa.[111]

On the minus side, while there are some Muslim organisations that support LGBT+ rights, same-sex relations are criminalised in all Muslim societies and for the most part extreme prejudice prevails throughout the Islamic world. The situation is likewise in many Christian societies, especially in Africa. In April 2019, the Sultan of Brunei caused global outrage for deciding to implement death by stoning as a punishment for homosexuality, though the scale of the condemnation eventually forced him to declare a (temporary) moratorium. To date, there remain over 70 countries where gay relationships are criminalised. Even in those more liberal societies seeking to promote LGBT+ awareness, resistance can be powerfully manifest, as has been with case with several schools in Birmingham, England, which are introducing LGBT+ inclusive lessons. The rise of the alt-right, especially in Eastern and Western Europe, has seen a dramatic increase in anti-LGBT+ hate crimes, leading to homophobic attacks on lesbians and gays. Illustrative of the rise in homophobia in Europe, in July 2019 the Polish ruling party declared 'LGBT-free zones' in Polish cities and provinces.[112]

Whether it suits the prevailing religious or political dogma or not, the reality is that we cannot switch off our sexuality. A person is straight or gay not by choice but by nature. And if you believe in God, then by His design. Not until it is ready to be switched off can our sexuality cease being the monkey on our back – unless you happen to be one of the 1% of the population who are asexual. This means that the vast majority of us must live with whatever sexuality we were born with, while experiencing and practising it in a prejudiced, pornified society which on the one hand is obsessed with every aspect of sex, commodifies it and makes it readily available to us in every conceivable format, but on the other hand tries hard to repress and control it.

The direction global society is heading with regards to sex and sexuality is not a healthy one, even if toxic masculinity continues to be challenged by women and some men. With the widespread introduction of robotic sex and sex dolls, discussed below, the opportunity for women and men to grow further apart is obvious.

This issue is additionally problematised by the way in which sexuality is caught up in generational tensions.

---

[111] https://www.nation.co.ke/news/Kenya-census-include-male--female-intersex-citizens-/1056-5212620-7k4fyz/index.html

[112] https://www.independent.co.uk/news/world/europe/poland-lgbt-free-zones-homophobia-hate-speech-law-justice-party-a9013551.html

Power and Innocence

Sexuality is not naturally toxic. It is entirely natural and should be made entirely welcome in our lives. It is a fundamental, indeed inevitable, part of being human, not just for reproductive reasons but for the unique experience of intimacy with another human being that it brings. But it becomes toxic when expressed as power and taken as entitlement.

From sexual harassment at an office party to gang rapes in a derelict tenement block, toxic masculinity enables. It is the primer for the act, the cultural enabler, the ideology behind the deed, the justification in the mind of the harasser, abuser, torturer or rapist.

Always, when examining toxic masculinity, we come back to this issue of power. It is present in all the dynamics which validate men's oppression of women and LGBT+ people.

The result is a loss of innocence. Sex and sexuality are no longer innocent, if they ever were. When male primary school children are being accused of sexual assault, older male children accused of rape, all children exposed to sexting, and adults adding to this toxic mess by being predators and abusers unable to give coherent and unified direction, sex has lost whatever innocence it once had.

I recently conducted a simple survey among pre-school and primary school teachers in Malaysia. The teachers were a mix of Bruneian, Malaysian, Chinese, Indian, Sri Lankan and Filipino. Many of them have a decade or two experience in education. When asked "what are the primary characteristics of Generation Z children?" one of the top responses was "growing up too fast, and loss of childhood".

Childhood is a lot shorter today than when I was a child in the 1950s. Children bullying each other in school in not new. Children having sex in school is. Children sexually assaulting and raping in school is. Children posting naked images of themselves on social media certainly is. At a recent Bangkok 'gender awareness' programme I delivered to 24 teachers and counsellors from the leading international schools in Thailand, one of the observations made and agreed on by all those present was that for Thai high school children (14-17), it is now 'normal' for a boy and girl to send each other naked photos before they start dating. It is expected. This observation was subsequently confirmed by the Thai women I interviewed for my research into their career and family aspirations. Parents of these children would very likely be horrified to learn just how wide the gap is between their image of their children's innocence and the reality of their children's sexualised behaviour.

Toxic masculinity not only feeds on power, prejudice and associated feelings of entitlement, it feeds on ignorance and denial.

How many parents are aware of the age at which their child first experiences a sense of their sexuality? For most children, it is 7-8. Around that age their sense of being straight or gay will be surfacing.

How many parents are aware of the likelihood their child will be LGBT+? Between 10% – 12% of children will be LGBT+, one in 1,500 children being intersexed.

How many parents are aware of how many sexes there are based on the most common chromosomes? There are six sexes, not two.[113]

How many parents are aware of the likelihood their LGBT+ child will get bullied at school? It is almost 100% sure any LGBT+ child will experience bullying as a direct consequence of their sexual and gender identity.

How many parents would openly accept their child to be LGBT+? Not many.

Toxic masculinity too easily fills the gap which gets created when adults retreat to their own sexual and gender binary comfort zones and prejudices.

Empowering Female Sexuality?

It is impossible to truly know how female and male sexuality was experienced down the ages; we weren't alive to experience it, so we are left with subjective perspective and interpretation. But we do know how sexuality is being experienced differently between the sexes around the world today.

> Hetero-sex as a mechanism by which men dominate women. Sex is about male dominance and female subordination. Hetero-sex as a display of male social, political, psychological and economic dominance over women. The expression of (hegemonic) masculine traits such as aggression, power and violence during sex shapes the meaning of sexuality for both men and women. Women therefore come to understand their role within hetero-sex as passive and accommodating.[114]

Dominant, traditional masculinity brings with it a particular understanding of men and women as differentiated agentic beings: e.g. man as the actor, women as the acted upon. Is this universally true? No. Women too are sexually agentic and always have been, while there have always been men who remain quietly sexually passive. That said, as the quote above argues, reflecting the views of radical feminists such as Andrea Dworkin, neither toxic masculinity nor the gender binary is designed to reinforce male acquiescence and female agency. Just the opposite.

How apparent is this differentiation today?

---

[113] https://www.joshuakennon.com/the-six-common-biological-sexes-in-humans

[114] Barber, K. (2011) 'Sex and Power', in *Introducing the New Sexuality Studies*. Chapter 7.

If we take another look at the Thai high school children exchanging naked images of themselves as a prelude to possibly dating, what and who's got power in that process? Do the girls willingly participate or reluctantly? Do they willingly accept that to have any chance of dating a boy they must succumb to what has quickly become the dominant expectation and code of behaviour, the rite of passage to sexual maturity?

Are the girls victims of toxic masculine behaviour or are they recognising and using their sexuality, expressing it as power? No longer confined to the velvet box of purity and stereotypical female innocence, female sexuality is revealed as not passive but very active, thereby overturning the toxic masculine discourse.

> *We live in a society where power and privilege lie in the hands of men. Patriarchy controls women and limits their freedom. Women are not, however, victims, not completely powerless. Women can use their sexuality to achieve liberation by exploring their own desires and sexualities and fully embracing sexual variety, so long as it is between consenting adults.*[115]

This quote reflects the other side of the feminist perspective and is argued by Pat Califa. For Califa, the key term is consent. But as I discussed in the previous chapter, when examining the motivations for the woman performing FGM on another woman, consent is a complex issue. The girl who sends the naked image of herself to boys in her school may think she is doing it consensually. But it could also be argued she is a 'cultural dope', unable to act outside the limitations imposed upon her by a society consumed by toxic masculinity. In other words, she is blindly complicit, compliant in her own sexual objectification for the pleasure of males. She does not cognitively choose to sexually objectify herself; she has internalised the options and subconsciously accepted to comply with the demands made by males with power over her, and by implication, power over her sexuality.

Consent

Of course, the complex issues around consent go both ways; they apply to males as well as females. Indeed, it is apparent that the era of MeToo, if it has done anything, has driven an express train through the previously 'understood' codes of behaviour that tended to prevail between men and women.

It is apparent from recent research, conducted by the American Family Survey (2018),[116] that what one considers to be sexual harassment differs according to both age and gender:

---

[115] ibid

[116] https://www.brookings.edu/events/the-2018-american-family-survey/

1. Most men do not consider a colleague looking at another colleague's private parts or asking for sexual favours as sexual harassment, while two-thirds of women say it is.
2. Almost a third of women think sexual jokes are harassment, while just 17% of men do.
3. Two-thirds of those aged 65 and over think that asking for a sexual favour always counts as sexual harassment, but the number falls to only about half for young adults aged 18-29.
4. Most respondents considered that consent should be sought before putting your arm around someone, 30% said not.

This gets even more complicated when we get to sex.

5. 67% said there must be verbal consent before having sex; 22% said non-verbal consent was acceptable; 6% said no consent was necessary.

A recent UK survey (2018) by the End Violence Against Women Coalition[117] found that a third of people think it isn't usually rape if a woman is pressured into having sex but there is no physical violence. A third of men polled believe that if a woman had flirted on a date it wouldn't be considered rape if she hadn't explicitly consented to sex. This view was held by only 21% of women. And almost a quarter of the 4,000 people questioned in the Attitudes to Sexual Consent survey carried out in the UK by Yougov (2018)[118] believe that sex without consent in long-term relationships was not usually rape. The UK law is very clear that it is rape.

Are these men right to be confused about what is and isn't appropriate behaviour towards women, or is this problem merely another example of a larger culture war emerging not just in the West but globally? Is men's confusion sincerely held or is it simply a screen behind which they are in reality hiding their frustration that the rules of male power and sexual expression are changing, maybe forever; a screen which all too easily turns out to be another factor in reducing the possibility of men changing, but also the possibility of intimacy between the sexes?

The consent issue merely illustrates how far apart men and women now are. Is this gap destined to widen or can men become wiser, more reflective, less hostile towards gender enlightenment, and indeed more enlightened about their own masculine assumptions?

[117] https://www.endviolenceagainstwomen.org.uk/

[118] https://yougov.co.uk/topics/resources/articles-reports/2018/12/01/publics-attitudes-sexual-consent

The AI variable

Of course, consent issues go out the window if you are a man who avoids women altogether. And increasing numbers of men are doing just that, especially in their sexual relationships.

Akihiko Kondo (35) recently married Hatsune Miku at a US$18,000 wedding ceremony in Tokyo. Nothing unusual about that, except that Hatsune is a 'piece of computer-generated singing software with the persona of a big-eyed, 16-year-old pop star who has long, acqua-coloured hair'.[119]

"I believe the shape of happiness and love is different for each person", said Akihiko.

You may consider this arrangement bizarre but it is becoming more common. There are already instances of American and Japanese men 'marrying' their sex dolls, while sexbot brothels are opening up around the world.[120]

Artificial Intelligence heralds dramatic changes in human intimacy, notably via the growth of such 'robotic relationships'. Although this trend is recent and at time of writing no 'fully functioning sex robots exist', already we are seeing how men can become seriously emotionally attached to a computer; a sexbot. They are apparently very happy to replace flesh and blood with a platinum/silicon device that can "hold a conversation" and imitate an orgasm. Perhaps this is because the docile and placid sexbot makes no emotional demands on the man? He can exercise total control over this 'female'; he can have as many varieties as he can afford; he can discard them as he wishes; he can treat them in whatever manner takes his fancy; he can enact any sexual fantasy; and he can switch them off when he's bored. This, for many men, is the perfect relationship.

Humans increasingly having sex with robots is most definitely a trend and with that trend will come an inevitable decline in male-female intimate relationships. For example, I fail to see how a man 'in love' with a sexbot and having regular sex with it, is going to make the effort to reflect on his masculinity, or indeed make the effort to connect with women. Likewise, I doubt many women will be keen to connect with him.

At the same time, it might 'solve the problem of the incel in society', by providing millions of lonely males of all ages and cultures with a sexual device that corresponds with their sexual fantasies, even if that fantasy is a replication of toxic sexuality in practice.

While AI still has a long way to go, already it has had the most dramatic impact on human relationships.

[119] https://www.japantimes.co.jp/news/2018/11/12/national/japanese-man-marries-virtual-reality-singer-hatsune-miku-hologram

[120] https://www.dailymail.co.uk/news/article-3754587/Sex-robot-brothels-commonplace-streets-Britain-says-professor.html

The 2019 'How Couples Meet and Stay Together' study by Stanford University found that 39% of heterosexual couples meet through online dating or apps, up from 22% in 2009, when the study was last conducted.[121]

AI is very much here, if not yet fully in our bedrooms, then certainly influencing who we end up in bed with.

When examining masculinity, and indeed femininity, we need to recognise that sexuality is the wild card; it is the most powerful of human emotions and physical feelings. None of us are in control of it; indeed for the most part it controls us.

[121] https://exhibits.stanford.edu/data/catalog/ns183dp7831

Part Four

Caves and Crossroads

Chapter Nine

(De)Toxifying Men

Looking at the world from a certain perspective, one might conclude it is not a good time to be a man. Yet measured by violent deaths, the world has never been more peaceful than it is today. Measured by increases in incomes, health, education and technology, the world has never offered more prosperity, security and opportunity than it does today. But measured by the rising power of women and the questions they are raising about male behaviour, the world has never been a more insecure place for men.

Should we, then, feel sorry for men caught as they are in the crosshairs of history?

During my research I've had many older Western men say to me; "I'm just glad I'm not 20 anymore. I think young men have a tough time of it, nowadays." Such comments are often followed by observations about modern women: "women seem harder than when I was a youth. They are the strong ones now, not the guys."

I think there is a lot of truth in this. Living in South East Asia, I see the same gap opening up between the aspirations of women and those of men as in the West. I see the same stark differences between the confident expressions of a new strident femininity and the ego-shrivelling anxieties of a masculinity that seems to have lost its way but is desperate to carry on as if nothing has changed.

At the same time I also see something else; disappointed women. They may be pursuing independence, freedom and choice, but it is leaving them alone. Most straight women don't want a life of singularity. And nor do most straight men. It is best for both sexes if they can live together, in harmony, in intimacy, and with mutual respect and equality.

But humans never have enjoyed that situation and we are certainly a long way from it right now. In fact, depending on how you choose to interpret the evidence, women and men have never been further apart than they are today.

Ever since I began my study of men and masculinities, some 30 years ago, I have tried to see gender dynamics in an historical perspective. It is too easy to get blinded by the spotlight of the present. We need to see not just what this spotlight reveals about this moment, but what it reveals about the past and might tell us about the future.

The past is, of course, another country, one we can never inhabit except through our imaginations and subjective interpretation, but nevertheless there can be little doubting the historical trend when it comes to gender relationships. Women are gaining power and inevitably men are losing it. Femininity has become a desirable trait, masculinity has become a problem. This is, without doubt, revolutionary both in its effects and in its implications. Indeed, in my opinion and that of many other observers, the gender revolution is the most profound and far-reaching to ever impact on humanity. What is particularly mesmerising is the pace by which it has occurred; its origins can certainly be traced back to the Age of Enlightenment, though it is the last hundred years, especially the last two decades, which have shaken the old gender order to its roots. To be sure, one must factor in a host of variables all of which have a direct bearing on this revolution, including medicine, health, education, technology, post-industrialisation, the media, globalisation, the information society and so on. And we must not forget the ongoing struggle of millions of women worldwide who find it hard just to survive in a male-dominated environment. But looking globally and historically we can see an unmistakable trajectory, which is for women to acquire more power, more confidence, more assertiveness and more independence from men.

This trajectory opens up several intriguing scenarios and these are explored in my final chapter. But before we get to those scenarios, something else must be attempted by global society: We must try to detoxify men from a masculinity which damages women, damages society and, not least, damages them.

Toxifying Men

Although masculine identity has never looked more precarious than it does today, we should not assume it has never been under a critical gaze. The fear of what men might do, what men might become, has been the sub-text informing much of the human story. One of the central aims of organised religion has always been to control men and their desires. Militarisation, leading to empire, weaponisation, conquest and war, has long been driven by the need to ensure a nation's menfolk do not 'go soft'; an 'heroic male project' that explicitly excluded women and any behaviour deemed 'feminine'.[122] The problematic relationship between men and a 'soft' masculinity was exemplified in the notion of 'muscular Christianity', where 'manliness was to be more openly 'not feminine' and more directly associated with physical strength, physical trial,

---

[122] See Whitehead, S.M. (2002) *Men and Masculinities*. Cambridge: Polity. Chapter 2

denial (of luxury) and 'endurance in the face of death and torment'.[123] This ethos defined the English public-school system and does so to this day. One of Hitler's over-riding concerns during the 1930s was to physically and mentally prepare the German men for war, so as to become his 'warriors of the master race' – he feared they were not sufficiently hardened to fulfil his dream of Aryan supremacy.[124] The Boy Scouts of America, formed in 1910, was designed explicitly to create a new generation of 'masculine males'.[125] Go forward a hundred years and today we have the Russian Orthodox Church claiming that "real men are being replaced by scrawny chickens" lacking traditional masculine values.[126] We have the US military establishment desperate to meet even a baseline recruitment target due to the fact that many young American men are either unwilling or unfit to serve in the military.[127] And we have the Chinese government openly encouraging schools to 'train boys to be men': because 'the alternative for Chinese boys (aged 7-12) is life in a society where androgynous pop idols, overprotective mothers, and mostly female teachers would turn them into effeminate cry-babies'.

> China's preoccupation with strong men has taken on a political dimension, feeding concerns about whether young Chinese males are in trouble. State media has said video games, masturbation, and a lack of exercise have made many young men ill-suited for the military. "Erasing the gender characteristics of a man who is not afraid of death and hardship is tantamount to a country's suicide".[128]

Whether the discourse circles around notions of 'feckless white working-class males'; a 'dangerous, criminalised sub-strata of ethnic minority men', the growing number of 'hapless men who are now the disposable sex', male 'religious fanatics', or simply 'hardening men up so they can be warriors', the reality is that males are seen as a problem. Their 'natural energies and impulses' need to be directed, and the direction society has chosen is toxic masculinity. But this trait is not natural to men; it has to be learned. And throughout history, males have been taught it. They are still being taught it. The appalling fact is that males have been sold the idea of masculinity as violence, aggression, conquest,

[123] Newsome 1961, quoted in Whitehead, 2002, Chapter 2

[124] Stargardt, N. (2015) The German War. London: Vantage.

[125] Whitehead, S.M. (2002) Chapter 2

[126] https://www.themoscowtimes.com/2019/04/15/weakling-chicks-are-replacing-real-men-russian-church-official-says-a65235

[127] https://www.armytimes.com/news/your-army/2018/09/21/the-army-is-supposed-to-be-growing-but-this-year-it-didnt-at-all

[128] https://www.scmp.com/news/china/society/article/2171040/inside-chinas-training-camps-where-boys-are-learning-how-be-men

dominance, selfishness and competitiveness, combined with repression of their deepest emotions.

This myth was sold to your father, my father, and all their fathers before them. Its consequences are all around us, from religious fanaticism to denial of global warming, from corrupt capitalism to the extinction of species, from rampant weaponisation to misogyny, from racism to homophobia, from empire building to genocide, and from domestic violence to male suicide. We have built a world on toxic masculinity, and humanity has paid the price. Humanity continues to pay the price.

In effect, society toxifies men. It does this through its rigid education systems, through its brutal judicial systems, through its uncaring political systems, through its divisive class systems, through its inherent militarisation, through its discourse of empire, through the myth of 'superman', through to the prevailing stereotypes of race, sexuality, and gender; it is embedded as much in the competitiveness of the global capitalist system as it is in the authoritarianism of modern Russia and China. We see it in the machismo of South America, and the brutal conflicts which continue to infect Africa. We see it in youth knife crime and in football hooliganism. We see it in the intolerant and radical versions of Islam, Christianity, Hinduism, Judaism and Buddhism. We can see it surface in America, a weaponised 'liberal democracy' that apparently needs to incarcerate over two million of its citizens and keep another 4.7 million on parole (93% of whom are male) in order to feel safe. And we see it in China, now desperate to stop its young males 'becoming sissies'.

The toxification of males starts early, from the moment they are born. It takes root in language and in practice, and feeds into men's expectations, self-perceptions and how they relate to women. We know this but still we seem unable, or unwilling, to stop it.

Victims

One of the easiest ways to control a young male is to put him in a uniform, tell him to stand to attention, listen to instructions, and then march up and down to martial music. Tens of thousands of schools around the world do this every day, usually first thing in the morning. I doubt the teachers realise what they are cultivating here, but for sure it is not healthy. This process of masculine toxification continues when the schoolboy goes home and his father tells him to 'stop being soft', to 'man up', to 'not act like a queer', to 'be tough', and for a treat this weekend 'we'll go hunting in the forest' or 'practising on the shooting range with my new rifle'. Twice a week, he'll go for sports training, where he's encouraged to 'get stuck in', 'toughen up', don't be a wimp, and constantly advised 'no pain, no gain'.

At school, the boy is bullied because he looks or acts a little 'soft'; maybe he likes to read books, is reflective, wears his hair a little too long and doesn't like sport. Anything which might signal his difference to the larger corps of males is dangerous. He gets excluded, isolated, knocked around a bit, and yet he tells no one. He internalises his pain, spending days and nights on the computer, submerging himself in a singular masculinist fantasy world of violent, misogynistic video games. Or he becomes the bully, surrounded by his mates, his gang; the validators of his slowly toxifying masculinity. Maybe the temptation to get into criminal activities, however minor initially, is too strong. The chance to exhibit bravado. The opportunity for further bonding with his mates. A sense of being and becoming a man.

If he is a little luckier, he'll be born into a middle-class family with a bit more money, disposable income, cultural capital and a stronger social safety net. He gets sent to an expensive kindergarten, an even more expensive primary school and eventually to an intolerably expensive international school. He could end up being a boarder, away from any family members for months at a time, exposed only to the school regime and, more riskily, the regime of his male peers. From the age at which he could understand, he's told to put education first, to do his homework, to never forget what he can be in life, to not relax, not play around too much, because his only aim must get himself into one of the few world-class universities.

From his earliest years he's being taught that life is competitive, and only boys who are strong, brave, and intelligent will make it. The rest are destined for who knows what? The future looks decidedly uncertain, even in primary school. The message is that boys are stronger, better and powerful, but then he asks himself why it is that the girls in his class always ask more questions, always get better exam results and always seem keener to study. Are we boys thick, or what? Is this what it means to be a boy? To be rebellious, a little stupid, a nuisance?

The females in his life are already marked out in his maturing mind as cleverer, different and desirable. But they are also 'the Other'. He must not be like them. They are the objects of a growing attraction; acceptable to be objectified, pornified, if he is straight. And if he is gay, then one only hopes he has some understanding friends and understanding parents.

By the time he reaches 18, he is either in higher education, or somewhere else. Where that somewhere else might be, who knows? It could be the armed forces, in which case toxic masculinity gets totalised – forever imprinted on his psyche. He will never fully escape that imprint. Or maybe he has graduated to hanging out with the street gangs, the older males dealing drugs, already on a path to an early death or imprisonment. If so, it is a path he will almost definitely follow, likely aided by a knife and gun. Possibly his dad is a cop, in which case he'll likely want to follow in father's path. Whatever path he chooses it won't make much difference: toxic masculinity in the criminal fraternity is absolutely no different to the toxic masculinity in the judicial system. They both feed on and nurture the same myths about what it means to be a man. They can both produce men who are repressed, aggressive and emotionally dysfunctional.

And if he is in university, having made it thus far through that complex maze called 'growing up' and into early adulthood, what has he got? Well, much depends on his relationship with his family, especially with his father. And at this point the key fork in his life materialises: into progressive masculinity or remaining stuck in toxic masculinity. It depends on so many factors, all of which are outside this growing child's comprehension, never mind control.

Are we really surprised that so many males are messed up?

It seems to me largely a matter of luck whether a boy ends up with a toxic masculinity or a progressive one. And luck is a rare commodity.

Society knows but conceals a terrible truth about boys and men; they are expendable. They are expendable as weapons of violence and aggression, they are expendable as workers, they are expendable as fathers. Which is ironic given the importance society accords to men over women. It is as if society needs to keep the myths of masculinity alive because to face the harsh truth, that men are victims of society's constant need for more male bricks in the wall, is just too unpleasant and damning.

But that is where we are now rapidly heading with toxic masculinity; exposing the fact that men are bricks in a wall, but one that no longer needs to be built. It is a wall without purpose but still we keep piling on the bricks. Global society is essentially driven by the same toxic masculine values that inhabit the minds of most men. But society just cannot keep the illusion going any more. The circle of self-sustained justification and validation is broken, and women have broken it, along with events. Twenty-first century events have exposed the contradictions, contagions, dangers and false promises inherent in toxic masculinity, a masculinity that must be taught to males if it is to take root in their minds. The problem now is that society is continuing to teach toxic masculinity, is still driven by toxic masculinity, but has no outlet for it when these toxic boys mature into toxic men. We only need so many soldiers, so many engineers, so many fighter pilots, so many tech wizards, so many F1 racing drivers, so many pro basketball players. We only need so many men in uniform. We can only build so many prisons.

Growing numbers of men are surplus to requirements. Society doesn't need them for marriage, for human reproduction, for economic growth or even for its safety and security. And AI is about to knock even bigger gaps in the wall. Men with toxic masculinity have nowhere to go. If they can learn to be reflective, adaptable and a little emotionally resilient, yes, they can possibly change. If not, then they are stuck. And the rest of us are stuck with them.

Reflections on a Journey

It is May 1991 and I am lecturing to a class of 28 Professional Football Association apprentices (16-17) at a Further Education College in Leeds, UK.[129] The apprentices are signed up with top regional football clubs, including Leeds, Sheffield, York and Bradford. Every FA club in the UK has such apprentices. This group comes to my college one day a week to do a BTEC Sport and Leisure programme. I am the programme director. The lads, most from working-class backgrounds, are always boisterous, full of energy, into practical jokes and only interested in kicking a football. They'd rather be anywhere than in my class studying sport and leisure. But they have no choice; it is a compulsory part of their two-year government-sponsored apprenticeship. Each is hoping to get a full contract with their club at the end of two years, and go on to become a pro footballer. A great life if they can manage it, but no more than one in 100 will do.

Their culture is heavily macho, with aggression and assertiveness precisely the traits the football clubs are looking for and indeed, which they encourage. They exist in a culture dominated by men; from the pro footballers to the club manager; from the physio to the club scouts; from the club owner to the club fans. These young men are already well imbibed with toxic masculinity; homophobic, competitive, physical, casually sexist and bullying of anyone showing any sign of weakness or femininity, even the lecturer. But they are likeable, despite all that. They have a youthful innocence around them, one not yet totally erased by the harsh demands of professional sport and its ruthless culture of winning above all else, with losers nowhere. And these lads mostly definitely fear being seen as losers. As a lecturer, you have to be above that culture, but in order to engage with the lads you cannot be too aloof. There is a fine balance to be struck and not every lecturer can handle it.

I can handle it, mostly, and the lads respect me not least because I am the director, with some influence over their future. But I am also at that time studying gender – men and masculinities – for my MA, so my lecturing becomes an opportunity for participant observation in hegemonic masculinity in sport. The lads definitely don't want to discuss their masculinity. After all, this is only 1991; it is twenty-five years before MeToo and the term 'toxic masculinity' gets invented and goes mainstream. But one afternoon, masculinity does come to the fore with astonishing consequences.

---

[129] Thomas Danby College, Hunslet, Leeds. Between 1987 and 1996 I was Programme Area Manager for Leisure, Sport and Tourism.

During this particular lecture one of the lads mentioned how his father had encouraged him to go into sport, especially football, but how he was also an absent dad, having left his mother when the lad was just 10 years old, leaving his mum to raise a family of five on her own, living in a back-to-back terraced house in a depressed part of Sheffield. I spotted an opportunity in this unbidden remark. I opened the topic up, asking the group how many of them had encouraging fathers and what role their fathers played in their lives. It was if I had pressed some invisible button in the group. It began hesitantly, cautiously, and with some reservations, but eventually most every lad contributed. And as the topic developed, so the theme went from encouraging fathers to absent fathers, to abusive fathers, to violent fathers, and finally, with several lads, to tears. The tears shocked me. I was wholly unprepared for this, for these were lads who only cried if they missed an open goal, though I did sense how emotional their responses were becoming the more they opened up about their mostly toxic relationship with their dads. The group drove the discussion, not me. I didn't discourage it but nor did I engineer it. They merely reflected on their dads' involvement in their lives and in so doing, they felt sad; they experienced pain.

One of my young apprentices from a previous year's group was a lad called Gary Speed. Gary was different to the norm. He was intelligent, sensitive, quiet, handsome and a gifted footballer. Not aggressive or macho in any way other than on the football pitch. Leeds United gave him a full-time contract when he was 18 and he went on to play professional football with Everton and Newcastle, on the way becoming the captain of the Welsh national football team. In 2010, he was appointed manager of the Wales team, the pinnacle of his professional career. He committed suicide a year later, at the age of 42. It was eventually revealed that Gary was one of four soccer players who killed themselves in later life, all of whom as children were coached by Barry Bennell, a 'devious paedophile' who preyed on young footballers. Bennell's toxic masculinity, combined with his sexuality, left many young boys "destitute, suicidal and addicted to drugs and alcohol." Gary was one of his victims.[130]

Over the course of the next two decades, as I went from being a college lecturer to a university professor, many opportunities for male reflectivity opened up with my students. And when they did, I invariably took them – as long as the individual and group appeared comfortable to do so. But I never pushed it. I had learned that here was a button of Emotional Mass Destruction, at least for men with toxic masculinity. And once that button got pushed, there was no going back. The button wasn't the cause of these men's anguish; it was

[130] https://www.theguardian.com/uk-news/2018/jan/17/gary-speed-one-of-four-players-coached-by-barry-bennell-to-have-killed-themselves

simply the trigger. And the words which trigger the emotional response are very simple indeed; "tell me about your childhood".

Confrontation

Any man with toxic masculinity will probably be like that because of his relationship or non-relationship with his father or another influential male figure. Looking back, it would have been surprising if those football apprentices did not react emotionally once they began reflecting on their dads. I went through precisely the same process when I began my own journey into feminism. Indeed, I recall my PhD supervisor insisting I inserted a section in my thesis on my father and reflections on my relationship with him. It was both liberating and salutary to do so. I think it fair to say that every male academic I have ever met, from whatever culture or nationality, who has studied gender, feminism, men and masculinities, has similarly gone through this process. There is no escaping it. There is no denying that which lies dormant but alive within us.

December 9th 2018 and Elon Musk, the CEO of the electric car company, Tesla, is being interviewed by Lesley Stahl, for the CBS programme, *'60 Minutes'*;[131]

Lesley: "You grew up in South Africa."

Elon: "Yes. I left when I was 17, by myself. I had a backpack of clothes and a suitcase of books. And that's it."

Lesley: "Did you have a happy childhood?"

Elon: "No, it was terrible."

Lesley: "Are you serious?"

Elon: "Yes."

Lesley: "Why was it terrible?'

Elon: "It was very violent. It was not a happy childhood."

Lesley: "I do know you were bullied at school."

Elon: "I was almost beaten to death, if you would call that bullied. And my father was emotionally abusive. My father had serious issues."

Lesley: "OK, so you didn't have a happy childhood.

Elon: "No."

Lesley inadvertently pushed Elon's button, and what followed has been described by commentators as an unexpected tearful "emotional traumatic outburst", made all the more poignant by the fact that billionaire Elon Musk is seen as one the era's most powerful men; the model Alpha Male. But Elon Musk has his own 'serious issues' and at time of writing is being sued by one of

---

[131] https://www.cbsnews.com/news/tesla-ceo-elon-musk-the-2018-60-minutes-interview

the British cavers who helped rescue 13 boy footballers and their coach from the Thai cave they were trapped in during June and July 2018. Musk repeatedly and publicly called the man a "pedo" apparently for no other reason than the caver criticised Musk's contribution to the cave rescue effort.[132,133]

Toxic masculinity needs to be confronted. It cannot be accepted as the norm in society. But to confront it can be dangerous and threatening. Vulnerable men have fragile male egos and can react aggressively to any question regarding their masculinity, to any inference that it their manhood is 'not strong, potent and powerful'. Even men such as Elon Musk, who are seen as archetypal males – 'warriors', 'heroes', 'kings', 'wizards', 'emperors' – are exposed once they start reflecting on their maleness, especially their relationships with fathers. If you want to understand men like Trump, Duterte and Putin, you first need to understand the impact their fathers had on their character. The clues are in the past, not in the present. The answer to why a man's masculinity is toxic is likely to be found in that man's childhood relationships with men.

Men, through history, have mostly started from a position of being comfortably ignorant, cocooned in a masculinist culture which posed no critical questions, raised no doubts as to men's power, potency, dominance and supremacy over women and all 'others'. This way of being has been reinforced in everyday culture since the first masculine myths got written.

But today this state of ignorance and unawareness is being challenged, questioned by the Other: women and LGBT+ people. It is getting raised everywhere, even on the *60 Minutes* programme. This is where society is at right now.

No man, if he is in any way plugged in to global information, can remain in that cocoon for very long. He is now being forced to face a new knowledge and a new way of seeing men and women. His masculinity is no longer sacrosanct, something to be guarded in the way footballers shield their testicles when facing a free kick. Money, status and power won't shield him from this. Neither will silence and self-imposed isolation. The question is not whether he's going to experience this confrontation, but how he is going to react when he does.

Searching for an Inner Hero

During the 1970s 'men's groups' started popping up in the UK and USA. They were the first thoughtful response by men to the questions raised by feminism and feminists, and to the serious challenges brought on by the dramatic changes in (male dominated) work. By the late 70s, there were many such groups, with

[132] https://www.usatoday.com/story/money/2019/05/10/elon-musk-trial-pedophile-comment/1172020001

[133] The British cave diver subsequently sued Elon Musk for defamation. Musk was found not liable in the UK court.

men using this opportunity to explore the 'hitherto mysterious world of their own emotions'. One UK participant was Andrew Tolson and he went on to write a book about his experiences, in the process becoming one of the first British men to seriously engage with a critical study of men and masculinities:

> We [men in the group] began to discover that we had no language of feeling. We were trapped in public, specialised languages of work, learned in universities or factories, which acted as a shield against our deeper emotional solidarities. When we talked about ourselves and our experiences these would be presented through the public languages in abstract formal ways.[134]

In Tolson's experience of men searching for a narrative by which to define themselves, a narrative beyond the limited and increasingly fragile parameters of paid employment and class identity, the men struggle to reflect on who they are as men. They have no language to express their feelings, insecurities and contradictions. They are emotionally illiterate. They can only see themselves as workers. And when that work identity is removed they are left 'incoherent', 'silent' and dangerously 'introspective'.

By the mid-1980s, this search by men for their 'inner self' had gathered pace. It was to lead to the formation of 'male retreats', where men-only groups took off for long weekends in the countryside, the forest or remote areas, the aim being to share experiences and intimacies with other men, surrounded by nature, sitting by campfires long into the night, banging drums, chanting, all the while reaffirming their 'deeply essential (natural) manhood'; the 'deep masculine parts of themselves that they believe they had lost'. Robert Bly's 1990 bestseller 'Iron John'[135] captured this moment, with Bly urging men to use these retreats as an opportunity to find their 'inner hero', their 'masculine archetype', to resurrect their threatened masculinity and 'get back in touch with their inner masculinity'. The 'Iron John' concept was a significant part of the growing 'men's rights movements' in the West during this period. This movement was explicitly and implicitly promoting the idea that feminism had 'gone too far' and was now leading to the emasculation of men, even to the extent of oppressing men.[136]

The objective of the men's rights movement, it seemed, was for 'liberated men to get in touch with their feelings, and yet still feel good about their status, power and privilege over others.'[137] In other words, men become more enlightened about their masculinity while nothing much changes in respect

---

[134] Tolson, A. (1977) The Limits of Masculinity. London: Tavistock. (pp.135-136)

[135] Bly, R. (1990) Iron John. New York: Addison-Wesley.

[136] See Whitehead, S.M. (2002) Men and Masculinities. Cambridge: Polity. Chapter 2

[137] Messner, M. A. (1997) Politics of Masculinities. London: Sage.

of them needing to hold on to their patriarchal power and whatever privilege arises from this.

This attitude is still around.

It is December 2018 and a UK company called 'Rebel Wisdom' has organised a retreat for men in a converted barn in rural Buckinghamshire. The two-day retreat and workshop called *'The New Masculinity'* involves 'metaphorically, going into a cave and confronting the monster inside, eventually returning home with the "treasure" – a more fully integrated personality". One participant is Tim (62). He describes the moment when the emotion came rushing out:

> *We prepare to go "into the cave" using controlled breathing to enter into a different state of consciousness. It is surprisingly effective. Adam lies on the floor. I put my hand on his chest so he can register my presence and support. Eventually, he squirms and arches his back and his hands curve into claws. He begins weeping and muttering and starting a dialogue with his father. Exclamations fill the hall. "Fuck you," shouts one guy, repeatedly at the top of his voice. Many others call out and sob. Adam is crying so much I find myself weeping in distress.*[138]

The cave is an apt metaphor for toxic masculinity; a place of protection but also isolation, a trap. Tim has been awakened to just how strong a trap he has been living in all his adult life. Behind the meditative techniques and emotional outpourings experienced by him and his fellow participants is the idea that men can become more 'kingly', more masculine and heroic in their search for and conquering of the 'monster in their cave'. The route to this apparently desirable state is self-reflection, recognising and accepting the pain within, and removing it, each participant aiming to realise "the man I want to be and what stops me getting there." Inevitably, relationships with other men, notably fathers, play a major part in this journey towards 'enlightenment'.

> *There is a final [day] of talking meditation in groups of six, each of us having to state what we appreciate about ourselves and what the others in the group appreciate about us. In my experience, although men banter and are capable of great compassion, they rarely directly compliment one another (women seem to do it naturally). To affirm one another without irony feels highly novel and very rewarding. When the other men in the group tell me what they appreciate about me, I find myself very moved. I realise I am not used to experiencing this kind of praise, from either gender. Men often survive in a culture of criticism. I don't think I am unusual in recalling a father who never praised me.*[139]

[138] https://www.bbc.co.uk/news/resources/idt-sh/What_I_Learnt_On_A_Men_Only_Retreat

[139] https://www.theguardian.com/lifeandstyle/2018/dec/15/the-search-for-my-inner-hero-a-modern-masculinity-retreat

These are men grappling with toxic masculinity. They may not use that term to describe their manliness, but the fact that they are unable to reflect, that they have weak emotional intelligence, high levels of emotional repression, and find intimacy with other men strange and disconcerting, confirms it.

Are these men to blame for their flawed masculinity? No. They didn't design it; it was designed for them. It was waiting for them at birth and they duly adopted it. The toxic masculine cloak was waiting to be worn and they wore it, believing it validated them as men in the process. Now, however, they want to unlearn it, divest themselves of it. At least these men sense there is a problem and are trying to address it. Somewhat inevitably, the two-day retreat leads to anger, tears, emotional outpourings and bitter reflections of inadequate, equally repressed, fathers.

But the problem remains. And it remains because of the missing link in all this. The missing link in both *Iron John* and in *'The New Masculinity'* – feminism.

Feminism is the Antidote

When most men are faced with the big questions put to them by women, questions which touch on their sense of masculinity, manhood and maleness, they either retreat or lash out. They rarely accept the premise of the question. Why? Because it will almost certainly relate to reflection, communication, control, power, authority, dominance, aggression and emotional illiteracy – vulnerability. Men will shy away from confronting their selves. It is much easier and safer to confront the Other.

Men going on retreat from women has likely always been a part of the male ritual of masculine validation. But for fifty years, specific retreats of the type described above have been emerging which are explicitly about how men manage their relationships with other men, with their children and with their loved ones; retreats which force men to acknowledge their masculinity, usually through painful realisation of the way they were messed up by their fathers. This appears, on the surface, to be a positive move, an opportunity for emotionally braver men to confront their unacknowledgeable demons and in so doing, release their 'inner hero'. But these men are still in denial. They may get emotional and angry with their fathers, but like my football apprentices from the 1990s, they still want to protect their inner masculinity. There is a limit to how much they want to change, as men. That is the problem.

There is only one way for men to cease being toxically masculine and that is to become a feminist; to fully and willingly embrace the central tenets of feminism. Anything less that this is simply denial; a fearful insecure man continuing to search for some stronger, more resilient, more archetypal masculinity – a pointless and harmful quest. In other words, it is a desire for change but one driven by fear, not by recognition and self-awareness. *Feminism is the only antidote to the toxic masculine virus.* If a man cannot accept being a feminist, if he cannot fully embrace gender and sexual equality, then he is making little or no progress in changing. He is still hanging on to notions of male power, male privilege and male exclusivity together with the gender stereotypes that inform them. All that toxicity has to go.

What practical steps can men take towards achieving some greater self-understanding and enlightenment, while at the same engaging with feminism in such a way that they too can see the sense in being a feminist and confronting the toxic masculinity within themselves?

Men Learning to Be Feminists

Men Learning to Be Feminists in London:

David Brockway has been manager of the Great Men Project since 2014. He and his team deliver workshops on gender equality to teenage boys in schools across London and the South East. The topics include sexual harassment, homophobia, pornography and consent. The objective of the Great Men Project is to help the boys reshape their masculinity from toxic to progressive, and this requires they firstly confront the sexist ideas and assumptions that have been planted in their minds since birth, and then move on to recognise and accept the central tenets of feminism.

> *We especially talk about masculinity and feminism and what it really means to be a man. Adult men don't talk about these issues very much, we want to get that conversation normalised starting at an early age... We help the boys explore [gender]stereotypes that might be in their heads and what causes these stereotypes. Where do the boys get ideas like it's weak for men to cry, or women are strong, men are weak? Most of the boys have never had conversations like this before. Some of our most powerful moments... are when boys have the opportunity through talking to each other to realise that some of these ideas that they think they know are actually a result of conditioning and the world around them... Apart from the litany of negative consequences [toxic masculinity] has for women and girls, there are also many negative consequences for men and boys and at the top of this list would be mental health and suicide... We find in our workshops that boys have a lot of difficulty expressing their emotions, accepting emotional vulnerability and admitting to any form of weakness. We encourage the boys to critique phrases such as "Man up" and "Take it like a man." Which are really say, boys don't cry and boys don't ask for help when they're feeling down. The phrase "Man up" is especially important for us. They are two words which put together mean absolutely nothing, but any man can tell you that when told to do so they know exactly what was expected of them at that time.*[140]

[140] https://www.bbc.com/ideas/videos/why-the-phrase-man-up-is-so-destructive/p06sdqg6

133

It is a tragic and horrifying fact that the vast majority of boys growing up today are doing so in a social environment ridden with damaging, dangerous gender and sexual stereotypes. Until this changes, toxic masculinity will remain the global dominant masculinity.

The damage starts early, certainly before the child gets to kindergarten, and it continues through the male's life. This makes the work that David Brockway and others like him are doing, arguably the most important intervention that can be made in any young man's life. It is a sight more important than getting them to university. Because if he and his team can succeed in weaning these boys off toxic masculinity and all it entails, getting them to be comfortable with describing themselves as 'feminists', then it is no exaggeration to say he will not only have enhanced lives, he will have saved lives: the lives of the boys themselves and the lives of those they connect with as adult men.

This can only be done in the context of feminism, not in the context of these boys going off and engaging in male bonding rituals that merely serve to reinforce their sense of being different to women. They must emerge from this process as feminists and active supporters of gender equality. And they won't achieve that by searching for some 'inner warrior' – this merely reinforces the very masculine stereotypes that need to be dismantled in their minds.

It is important not to 'sell' this to boys and men as yet another extension of the mythical heroic project that informs toxic masculinity. Males have to go beyond that if they are to let go of the thinking that has hitherto informed their relationships and their sense of self.

As David Brockway says, "*we need to teach boys to be feminists.*"

Men Learning to Be Feminists in Beijing:
"The penis!" nine men answered together.

"What do you call your penis?" the man asked again.

"Birdie." "Tea Kettle." "My precious." "Cock." "The thing," the other men answered one by one.[141]

The audience are stunned into silence, not a murmour, not a word; 'they hold their breath, listening intently'. This is an opening scene of *The Penis Monologues*, a play performed at the French Embassy in Beijing in early December 2018 and written by Fang Gang, feminist and 'renowned sexologist and professor' at Beijing Forestry University. Fang had watched Eve Enslers' play *The Vagina Monologues* more than 10 years earlier and was 'blown away'. He decided to do a male version that was essentially feminist in its objectives: challenging violence and discrimination by men towards women, but from the perspective of men. The monologues are based on true stories which Fang has

[141] https://www.scmp.com/news/china/society/article/2177041/how-chinas-penis-monologues-are-trying-detoxify-masculinity

gathered from Chinese men during years of research into men and masculinities in China. The actors go through the actual dialogue used by such men, creating powerful vignettes of male violence, rape and abuse towards women, as well as homophobic bullying.

> *When my penis entered her body, I was overcome with ecstasy. She is finally mine... it's like I put a stamp on her body, a label that marked by sovereignty... [Years after] I realised I had date raped her... when I was raping her, I satisfied my need for control, occupancy and conquest, not love. I thought I loved her, but I didn't respect her choices.*

The Penis Monologues was launched by China White Ribbon, a group created by Fang in 2013, which aims to provide counselling to male domestic abusers so as to change their behaviour.[142] Fang's work, and that of China White Ribbon, is 'dedicated to challenging traditional masculine stereotypes', stopping domestic violence and encouraging more Chinese men to embrace feminist values.

> *The symbol of a man isn't the penis. The pride of a man isn't an erection. 'Man' should not mean 'violence'. A good man doesn't need to be macho and hegemonic, doesn't need to be sexually active. They can do housework, can take care of their children, can say no to violence and can respect diversity and promote gender equality.*

Men Learning to Be Feminists in South Africa

In any list of the most violent places on earth, South Africa invariably makes it into the top 20. In any list of the most dangerous countries for a woman to live, South Africa invariably makes into the top 10. Indeed, a recent survey of 4,000 South African women revealed one in three had been raped. This fits with a similar survey of South African men showing 25% of them admitting to rape; of those, half said they had raped more than one woman.[143]

If any country was in desperate need of feminism, it is South Africa.

It is a warm Saturday afternoon in Pankop, a small town in Eastern South Africa. A dozen young men and teenage boys are seated in a circle in the yard of a friend's house. They are gathered twice a week to talk about women, respect – and sex. The group has been formed by Kabelo Chabala, founder of the Young Men's Movement. He is one of a growing number of men fighting toxic masculinity in South Africa.

> *The talks centre around positive masculinity, being a better generation of men and talking about the challenges we face as men in the midst of being sidelined... There is a lot of toxic masculinity in this country {and a lot of this] is down to many young men in South Africa growing up without good role*

---

[142] http://en.people.cn/n3/2016/1118/c90000-9143776.html

[143] ww.marieclaire.co.za/hot-topics/new-study-on-violence-against-women-south-africa

models. I realised that growing up without a father figure in my life could have influenced me to make some bad decisions. Many of these young boys don't have fathers that are present.[144]

Like the rest of the world, South Africa is experiencing a crisis of (toxic) masculinity, leading many men to become even more violent and aggressive towards women. This realisation spurred Chabala to launch the Young Men's Movement in 2015, its aim being to provide 'safe spaces' for men to talk about their feelings. These safe spaces enable men to explore otherwise 'taboo' gender and sexuality topics in a culture where a vicious form of hegemonic masculinity has taken root and where any men who deem to be 'different' are immediately rendered vulnerable.

Teaching these men to respect women is a crucial part of our aim. It is about working towards the liberation of their thinking, them accepting certain concepts in a progressive way. These safe spaces for men to talk about their feelings regards women and sex, are designed to create a safe environment for women in our country.[145]

Men Learning to Be Feminists in Spain

A man with toxic masculinity has no real friends. His is a life of solitude, a life spent fearful of inner emotions, a life spent forever hiding, a life spent behind a masculine mask. He has no true friends because he is forever pretending to be someone he isn't.

A group of Spanish middle-aged men recognise all that, which is why they choose to be part of the Fresh Wind men's group. Once a month, these men meet at the La Solana farm, six kilometres outside of Aracena, a small town in the southwestern Spanish province of Huelva. Fresh Wind men's group is one of hundreds of such groups now operating in Spain and part of a resurgent feminist movement across the country, fighting gender violence and supporting the demands of women against sexism. These men do not see feminists and feminism as the enemy. They recognise themselves as male allies in the feminist cause.

The men spend two hours talking, sharing their thoughts, sharing their fears, sharing their hopes. All conversations are confidential and only two topics are banned: sport and politics. Each month the group agree a new topic for discussion. On this particular evening the topic is about caregiving, 'an invisible job that is poorly paid, if paid at all, which women do twice as much as men', according to Spain's National Statistics Institute.

---

[144] https://edition.cnn.com/2018/12/21/health/south-africa-male-group-toxic-masculinity-intl/index.html

[145] https://rekordeast.co.za/111618/mentors-want-to-see-exceptional-men

This group of men has talked about everything from their sons and daughters, to their mothers and fathers, a difficult topic that lasted more than one session. They've also spoken about the women in their lives, their sexual feelings, their friends who never discuss personal matters, and of the "masculine solitude" that many men cannot even recognise.[146]

These men may not have been taught by their fathers to be open about their feelings, especially with other men, but once they start talking, the words tumble out; the emotion flows but in a positive way; the inner feelings, so long hidden and unresolved, surface.

"I have never taken care of myself or cared for anyone"

"When someone treats me with care I feel good"

"Until the last second, my father didn't allow himself to be vulnerable"

"What I fail at is tenderness"

"I heard you say tenderness. And I ask myself, when was the last time I spoke with tenderness?"

"I've never talked like this before."[147]

When feminist women get together, they invariably focus on self-empowerment. When feminist men get together they inevitably focus on exploring their feelings, especially their relationship with their fathers.

Men Learning to Be Feminists in El Salvador

In El Salvador, a woman is murdered by a man every 18 hours, giving this country of 6.5 million people one of the highest femicide rates in the world. Despite having the world's second-highest imprisonment rate after the USA, El Salvadoran men continue to adhere to toxic masculine behaviour, resulting in a culture of violence which borders almost on civil war. But it is a war the government is not winning, with an estimated 95% of gender-based crimes going unpunished, partly because of under-reporting.

Recognising that jail time for violent men is not preventing the soaring rates of gender violence, Benjamin Bonilla, director of Masculinities for Peace, a San Salvador-based NGO, introduced masculinity courses for violent offenders in prison. Support by the El Salvadoran judicial system, the programme has been extended to masculinity workshops for police, judges and investigators for the attorney general's office.

We [men] are the ones who are creating most of the violence in general and in context of violence against women... Because of the socialisation and construction of gender, we hold the belief that we do work with aggressors,

[146] https://elpais.com/elpais/2019/02/26/inenglish/1551174721_895648.html

[147] ibid

because we are all aggressors under this socialisation... If the system teaches boys from a young age this idea of superiority over girls, there is an aggressive idea starting there.[148]

"We aren't just going to use the traditional mechanisms, such as prison sentences, fines or volunteer service, that won't focus on transforming a person's patriarchal behaviour", says Glenda Baires, one of the two head judges of the specialised court.

Mario is one man who went through the masculinity transforming process while spending six months in prison for threatening behaviour towards his ex-girlfriend.

I used to be an aggressive, domineering and an arrogant person. Often a person doesn't see that they are carrying out some type of violence, and in the [masculinity awareness] class, they make us see it... The classes have helped me identify with how my behaviour embodied toxic masculinity.[149]

From London to Beijing to South Africa, El Salvador to Spain, the world is changing fast, and increasing numbers of men are waking up to what it means to have a penis and to use it as a weapon of oppression; what it means to believe that women are there to be pornified and abused; what it means to believe that 'men don't cry'; what it means to assume that men are the superior gender, and what it means to believe that homosexuality is a disease. For many such men, the journey will indeed end with full embracement of feminism. However, to imagine this process of self-enlightenment will be always be welcomed, linear and smooth would be a big mistake.

But once a man can be confronted with his toxic masculine attitudes and behaviour and accepts the need to change, then taking the next step toward profeminist attitudes is a lot easier. But making that first step is the key one. In other words, how to get men out of their TM cave.[150]

---

[148] https://www.aljazeera.com/indepth/features/male-aggressors-el-salvador-prison-masculinity-class-190330001520333.html

[149] ibid

[150] For men learning to be feminists in India go to http://www.mavaindia.org (Harish Sadani)

Chapter Ten

Emerging from the Cave

Our distant ancestors treated caves as places of shelter, protection from both the elements and wild beasts. There are caves around the world that were inhabited continuously for tens of thousands of years, through extended periods of human prehistory. The cave itself was not threatening, it was the world beyond that was dangerous. Toxic masculinity is such a cave; inviting, available, protective, but ultimately a dangerous illusion. Some men live near the surface, most are somewhere in the middle reaches, others are dwelling in the far depths, lost to male fundamentalism.

Society is faced with two tasks. One is to try and retrieve those men lost in the cave of toxic masculinity. The second is to ensure current and future generations of young males don't enter it.

The Five Levels

If you have ever studied or experienced 'culture shock'[151] then you'll likely be aware of the five progressive stages one might experience:

1. Honeymoon (euphoria and excitement)
2. Disintegration (feeling frustrated, discontented, angry)
3. Confusion (mixed feelings of pulling away and being drawn in)
4. Reorientation (adjustment, ability to function)
5. Adaptation (comfortable, engagement)
6. Biculturalism (assimilation, belonging)

Men emerging from the toxic masculinity cave experience a form of culture shock. With one notable difference – there is no honeymoon stage.

1. Aggressiveness (aggressive, misogynistic, angry towards feminists)
2. Anxiety (uncomfortable with feminism and MeToo, defensive, distancing)
3. Awareness (painful realisation mixed with confusion and uncertainty)

---

[151] Ward, C. Bochner, S. and Furnham, A. (2005) *The Psychology of Culture Shock*. London: Routledge.

4. Acceptance (comfortable, orientated towards feminist values)
5. Assimilation (declared feminist, practising feminist)

1. Aggressiveness: Men at this first level are at the very end of the cave, stuck in its furthest, darkest reaches. This is where they have ended up and this is where they intend to stay. There is nowhere else to go, no further to retreat. Men have been living here throughout history, comfortable in their self-imposed world of 'male supremacy', feeding on misogynism, notions of male power and the identity validation they get from the emotional and physical abuse of women and gays. Now, however, they are being disturbed by feminism, equal opportunities, gay rights and all that 'politically correct nonsense' they so vehemently hate. The incels, the male fundamentalists, lurk here and it will take a lot to shift them. Feminism and feminists are an easy target and they'll take aim wherever possible, with violence always an option. In their hierarchy of loathing, feminists are at the top, followed closely by LGBT+ people. There is an acute fear behind the defensiveness and the aggression. I was recently asked this question by a man trapped at this stage: *"What will happen when feminism goes too far in making men's lives unbearable?"*. This question reveals the other significant response by men stuck at the end of the cave and that is 'victimhood'; in their minds they are the victims of feminism, if not of all women – not the other way around. Whether or not a man can move off this level and up to the next largely depends on his willingness to let go of this sense of being a victim. None of these men will be able to make that start without help. And these men definitely need help; they are at high risk of depression, social isolation, suicide and violence. (key words: fear, resistance, homophobia, hate, defensiveness, anger, crisis, rejection, victimhood, misogynism).

2. Anxiety: This is where the vast majority of men with toxic masculinity tend to be. They are not aggressively anti-feminist, but they are definitely uncomfortable with it. In fact, they are also rather anxious about MeToo, LGBT+ rights and indeed the very topic of toxic masculinity. They feel increasingly confused and uncertain, especially in their dealings with women; they recognise the old rules of male/female behaviour have gone but they're not sure what has replaced them. They are aware of the movement towards empowering women and LGBT+ people, but they either want nothing whatsoever to do with it or they see themselves as not needing to engage with it. Some will probably imagine they are progressive enough. Others will have been living in their toxic cave for so long they've gone blind and can see no way of ever venturing out. These men take toxic masculinity as a term invented by feminists and, as such, a term that doesn't refer to them. As much as possible, men at this stage will distance themselves from feminists and instead ensure they are surrounded with like-minded men, using masculine bonding rituals, casual sexism, religious dogma, homophobia, perhaps even racism, to 'secure' their traditional masculine identity. They may join brotherhoods deliberately designed to exclude any 'Others'. They are blind to their masculinity and unreflective of their social conditioning. Many will be feeling a sense of crisis; depressed and socially isolated. Some will even be suicidal. However, there is another trait many of these men have which might just help them – curiosity. They are intellectually curious or, at the very least, willing to consider alternative viewpoints. This is positive, because these men have to face the big two questions: 1. 'what do I have to gain from questioning my masculinity?' 2. 'what do I have to lose?'. How they answer those questions determines whether or not they start the journey out of the cave. Often the journey gets triggered by a traumatic awakening; the pushing of their 'button'. (key words: uncomfortable, frustrated, disorientated, defensive, awkward, insecure, uneasy, confused, resisting, unreflective, curious).

3. Awakening: The recognition, the awareness that a man at this level experiences is quite simply that women may have a point, that perhaps there is something in his masculinity and gender worldview which might not be altogether healthy, either for him or those around him. The men in the *'New Masculinity'* bonding weekends reached this level in two days; not yet feminists but at least more conscious of their gender identity. Maybe for the first time in their lives they realised they had a masculinity, that this masculinity did have an impact on how they lived as a man, and that its impact was not wholly positive. Men at this level are at last recognising there might be a problem; they have woken up from a lifetime's slumber in the cave though still unsure as to where this new awareness actually takes them. This can create more confusion, leaving them unsure, hesitant and disorientated, but at least they do have a new knowledge and that won't be easily got rid of. This experience of heightened self-awareness can be a great relief for these men; they realise the world is out of order, not them. But they can also experience profound trauma and grief, for they must face the realisation that their way of being a man has been conditioned by society and they've paid a high price as a consequence: the absent, unloving father; the loss of love of a partner or a child; social isolation; depression; relationship break-ups and mental health problems. It is a lot to handle and it can be very painful. Some may quickly retreat further back into the cave, back into anger and defensiveness. Others may succumb to depression, faced – as they see it – with a dismal future where men like them are surplus to social requirements. One hopes that most will persevere and be curious enough about their maleness and their masculinity to want to unpick it, to go further. A lot of men will simply stick at this level, unable or unwilling to go on. Others will feel pulled in both directions – back to the familiarity of the cave and onwards into a new unknown. As they try and deal with these mixed emotions at least they now have a better understanding of what they have to gain by continuing, while being increasingly aware of what they have to give up. (key words: trauma, regret, sadness, confusion, pain, realisation, grief, displacement, recognition, relief).

4. Acceptance: Men at this level have reached the point of being willing to adjust their world view towards a feminist perspective. They still won't feel fully comfortable about adopting the label feminist, but they will no longer be fighting feminism. Nor will they be experiencing feelings of anger, confusion or uncertainty. They do not see women and feminists as the enemy and they will very likely adopt a positive approach to LGBT+ rights. This doesn't mean they are going to be joining any gay rights parades anytime soon, but they are in a much healthier place than before. They are almost out of the cave. They can see the light. They have gone through a lot of soul-searching, self-analysis, painful reflection and resistance. They are not the same men they were when they started the journey. They will have left many of their previous male friends behind, though almost certainly found new ones. A lot of men stick at this stage. And that is understandable because in many respects it is a compromise stage. However, while they accept the central points of feminism, there is still another level left for them: to put those central points into practice in their everyday life. (key words: understanding, adaptation, embracing, reflecting, acknowledgement, empathy).

5. Assimilation: Men who reach this final stage are out of the cave and embracing progressive masculinity. They can decide what sort of feminist they want to be, which aspects of feminism they take up or discount, but fundamentally they are allies of women in their quest for gender justice and they are pro LGBT+ rights. They are also anti-racist. It took me a while to get to this stage – I was very comfortable in my cave and stayed stuck in level four. Moving from theory into practice is hard, especially for a man like myself; a man whose masculinity mostly developed during the 1950s and 1960s. I know younger men very close to me who are at level five already. It is in their practice, the reason being they never entered the cave in the first place. For those men who are deep in the cave, getting to this stage won't be easy. The best analogy I can give is culture shock: everyone who goes to live abroad experiences it but very few become 100% assimilated into their new culture. To be a progressive man means precisely that, to be so assimilated with feminism and feminist values that you no longer think about it. It is who you are. It defines your masculinity and your relationship to everything and everyone around you. (key words: practising, engagement, supporting, enabling, belonging, feminist, ant-racist, enlightened).

These five stages equate to five levels of gender awareness, each one a step towards the ultimate objective, which is a man with progressive masculinity. But this process is neither linear nor straightforward. Some men will get stuck at a level and not proceed further. Others may actually slip back, especially if they experience rejection from women and men close to them. Stage two is the critical stage; this is where a lot of men are and we need to help them move on from that. Factors such as physical health, ageing, family relationships, romantic relationships, sexuality, career, education, work, social and cultural capital all conspire to also play a part. I doubt I would have reached progressive masculinity without encountering feminists during my MA in 1990, together with the emotional support of significant female others. I may have got so far towards the exit by myself, but the impulse to go further was provided by them. My intellectual curiosity then took over, persistently driven by my toxic relationship with my father.

The task facing society is to reach out to these men and help them exit their cave. This can be achieved in many cases but it will be a long, slow journey and large numbers of men alive today will never make it, partly because they have no desire to, but also because the process is too threatening, too out of kilter with the men they have become. But as more and more men do engage with feminism and encounter pro-feminist activities such as China White Ribbon, the Good Men Project[152] the Young Men's Movement and the Great Men Project, then some positive change is inevitable. This will not be men driving change, it will be men responding to the women already out there who are driving it. Men becoming feminists is always and inevitably about men following women on that journey, not the other way around. Women are the ones who take the lead on this. Men must be vocal but supporting actors. As more women become feminists and continue to expand a global feminist narrative, so will more men align with them.

But to imagine it will be done without emotional trauma is to fail to recognise what actually compels men to stay in the cave in the first place. That compulsion is driven by fear and insecurity; fear of being a different kind of man; fear of not being accepted by your mates; fear of recognising how unpleasant were your actions and behaviours in the past; fear of facing up to the damage you've done to women, to loved ones, to children; fear of losing power; fear of letting go of some very persuasive belief systems; fear of engaging with one's deepest emotions, and fear of accepting one's failure as a man.

The leaving of toxic masculinity for progressive masculinity is akin to jumping off a cliff after someone has told you there is a safety net at the bottom, albeit one you cannot see.

---

[152] https://goodmenproject.com

You have to trust this is a good way for you to go; you have to believe that you can be a better man than you are, and you need enough strength of mind to recognise this is the right call, regardless of what happens next.

What to Gain by Exiting the Cave

Accepting that the ultimate reason for all men to embrace progressive masculinity is to make the world better, safer, more peaceful, more enlightened and more sustainable, I will instead focus on the benefits to the individual man who makes this journey.

First there are the material benefits: 1) It makes him more employable in those organisations which see themselves as progressive. 2) It enables him to be a better team worker, manager and leader thereby helping ensure his upward career trajectory. 3) It means he will be comfortable with having a female boss and this in turn should translate into his ability to contribute to the organisation. 4) It will help him avoid toxic behaviours such as criminality, violence, venality and anything likely to result in him being caught up in the criminal justice system. 5) It will improve his educational attainment by several fold, leaving him much more likely to go to university and graduate with a good degree. 6) He is much more likely to be able to embrace globalisation and benefit from the opportunities it offers; this in turn means he will be able to function in society as a 'global citizen', having acquired the liberal mindset that identity demands.

Second are the relationship benefits: 1) It helps him relate to women and in so doing, improves his chances of having a long-lasting relationship. 2) It will help him understand his own parents, especially his father, and this in turn means he acquires a greater appreciation of himself and his role as a son and as a parent. 3) It will expand his friendship group and not limit it to men who are toxic themselves. 4) It will make him a more considerate, understanding father, thereby drastically reducing the chances of him continuing the toxicity into a new generation.

But the really important benefits come not from the externalisation of progressive masculinity, but from the internalisation of its core traits:

1. Improved emotional intelligence
2. Reduction in feelings of anger and aggression
3. Absence of hatred
4. Absence of misogynism, homophobia and racism
5. Absence of violence
6. Empathy
7. Improved wisdom and understanding
8. Improved self-confidence and self-esteem

9. Reflexivity and self-awareness
10. Reduction or elimination of depression
11. Stronger sense of identity, one not linked to masculinity but to humanity
12. Greater awareness and appreciation of femininity and the female condition
13. Sensitivity
14. Contentment
15. Reduction in feelings of confusion and identity crisis
16. Reduction in feelings of anxiety and emotional disruption
17. Reduction in suicidal feelings
18. Heightened emotional self-control

All of the above are important to the mental health and emotional well-being of a man, and all the above will benefit women and the rest of society. But arguably the most important trait in this list is *empathy*. If a man has empathy for others then it makes it nigh impossible for him to kill, murder, torture, abuse or hate. In other words, men with empathy don't put people in gas chambers. They don't hang them by their feet and subject them to electric shocks. They don't go around in gangs terrorising people. They don't rape and violate. They don't stab their girlfriends or wives when they say they're going to leave them.

In short, men who make the effort to exit the toxic masculine cave are not only doing women – indeed the whole world – a favour, they are doing themselves one also. It is no exaggeration to state that this is a journey of out of danger and into safety. And it is one which most men are capable of. If they so choose. The man who embraces progressive masculinity is, indeed, a better man. Not only is he non-toxic himself but he is more likely to be an advocate for change; a man who can himself help other men undertake their own journey.

How to Avoid Going Deep Into the Cave

Can a man avoid the cave altogether? Only if he is raised in a non-toxic way. Only if his parents are progressive and enabling of him becoming a progressive man also. Otherwise, he is probably fated to enter it. It is all down to upbringing; who his parents are. Biology doesn't enter the equation at all. And nor does race, ethnicity, nationality, money, class, sexuality or social status. Progressive masculinity is not incumbent on having a large bank account, a secure job or being loved by a succession of beautiful women. It is entirely in the mind of the man and is reflected in his core values, his ethics and his principles. In other words, it is almost impossible for a young male to avoid toxic masculinity if he has been raised in a social environment that brutalises him, feeds him ideologies of hate and discrimination, surrounds him with gender and sexual stereotypes, and effectively propels him towards a limited and outdated form of masculine identity. Certainly, education helps a lot and this experience, especially of higher education, can go a long way to ameliorate even the most toxic upbringing. It happened to me, and in my thirty years as an educationalist I have seen it happen to many other men. But I was in my 30s before my educational journey began. Most men with toxic masculinity are well into the cave long before then.

And what about the man who is in the middle reaches of the cave; how does he avoid slipping into the depths? Assuming that he is an adult man and not a boy, and therefore fully responsible for his own actions, then the man must avoid the temptation of hate. Hate is a virus and it feeds toxicity, it feeds feelings of isolation and frustration, and it draws strength from feelings of victimhood. Hate does not discriminate. A man might believe he can justify hatred of someone he sees as 'evil', but that hatred is not rational. It is a wild card emotion, beyond his control: it can and will spread into other areas of his life if he is not careful. An example would be a man who suffers grievous emotional pain from a relationship break-up while in his late teens or early twenties. He can see no reason or rationality for the woman leaving him and his grief is almost unbearable. But rather than compartmentalise this emotion and reflect on what she is feeling, the pain feeds into his everyday thinking and eventually his attitudes towards all women. He goes from loving one woman to hating them all. This may sound bizarre to many women but it happens all too often. Another central force driving a man down into the depths of toxic masculinity is when his desire to be a man gets brutalised. For example, a 14-year-old male at school finds the path to progressive masculine identity impossible to follow because it would serve to isolate him from his male peers. Encouraged by his peers and fearful of being bullied himself, he starts distancing himself from the education system and from authority figures in his life. Instead, he gravitates towards the male brotherhood groups operating in the school and/or in his neighbourhood. The opportunity for validation as a 'man' is just too tempting and he takes it, even if this means his eventually exclusion from school, his incarceration in prison or his early death. The only way to help men such as these is through specific interventions in their lives, helping them awaken to their toxic masculine value system while showing them there are better, healthier and safer ways of being a man. During the early noughties I was privileged to witness such a male mentoring programme get established in Manchester, UK, by Dr Richard Majors. Richard was a US sociologist who had written extensively on black male identity.[153] He recognised how vital it was for young men at risk to have positive male mentors in their lives. Richard

[153] Majors, R. (2001) 'Cool Pose: Black Masculinity and Sports, in S.M. Whitehead and F.J. Barrett (eds) *The Masculinities Reader.* Cambridge: Polity.

trained older men to be positive mentors, often men who themselves had been gang members and in prison. This is exactly the sort of intervention which is needed and which is now being replicated around the world with the likes of the Great Men Project, Masculinities for Peace, the Young Men's Movement, Men's Association for Gender Equity, China White Ribbon and the Good Men Project.

Does this mean that men with toxic masculinity are victims of it? Yes, up to a point. All men with toxic masculinity will suffer in some way or another as a consequence; for example, in broken relationships, mental health issues, depression, lack of empathy with others, behaving abusively or caught up in the criminal justice system. No human is in total control of their environment and especially not their upbringing. However, any man who has ventured deep into the TM cave, usually in search of a 'strong man' identity or in retreat from feminism, has done so largely by choice. He knows violence is wrong. He knows picking up a weapon and destroying another person's life is wrong. He knows jealousy, aggression and hate are toxic emotions that are corroding his inner peace of mind. He knows there are better ways of being a man. But for whatever reason, out of fear, anger, frustration, revenge, or just to feel good about himself, he has rejected empathy and understanding in favour of hate and anger.

I say to the misogynists, the racists, the homophobes, the rapists, the murderers and the abusers: You are where you are because you chose to be. You can choose to be a better man and you know it. You know how to be a better man. What happens to you from hereon is a consequence of the decisions you make in life, no one else.

How Do I Stop My Baby Boy Acquiring Toxic Masculinity?

The biggest challenge facing parents of boys is not so much ensuring they become wealthy in life or even physically healthy, but ensuring they do not grow to adulthood and become a danger to women. Secondly, that they do not grow to adulthood and become a danger to anyone else. Thirdly, that they do not grow to adulthood and become a danger to themselves. In short, do you want your son to be a victim of toxic masculinity or do you want him to become a smarter, healthier man?

If your answer is the latter, then you must prepare for this long before the birth of your son, assuming you know the child's sex. Indeed, even before conception. And you do so by you and your partner agreeing on the whole principle of progressive masculinity as the objective for your son. This masculinity will fit him perfectly well regardless of his educational attainments, regardless of his social class and especially regardless of his sexuality.

Don't assume anything about his sexuality – let him experience it, develop it and explore it for himself. By the age of eight, he'll have a good inclination of where his interests lie and you and your partner should be open to whatever emerges here. No judgements, no steering, no gender and sexual ideologies.

Of course, you may decide to go the route of an increasing number of parents in the West which is not to reveal the child's sex until the child is older. This is one way of helping ensure that the child develops outside the gender binary, fashioning their own distinct feminine/masculine traits as they so desire. Similarly, you can choose a gender-neutral name. My second wife and I did this with our child.

Use gender-neutral language as much as possible, always avoiding any phrases which signal boys as being different from girls, especially emotionally. Boys are not stronger, not tougher, not more active, not more emotionally closed off than girls. No comments such as 'that's so gay', no 'man ups', no 'don't be a sissie'. This serves two purposes: it again diminishes the corrosive effects of the gender binary in your child's life by reducing the likelihood of him seeing himself through a narrow masculine lens, and it also helps ensure he respects people for who they are, not for what they look like nor indeed for what genitalia they have.

Allow your boy to be who he is and express that in any way which suits him, as long as it is respectful to others. Don't try and force him into gender social conformity. An example here is Aaron Gouveia's son, Sam (5). Apparently, Sam likes to paint his nails in bright colours. He also likes sports and playing with trucks. However, Sam was bullied at his Massachusetts kindergarten precisely because he loved his pink fingernails. Aaron's response to this was a classic and quickly went viral:

> Sam was ridiculed for being a boy with nail polish. They called him names and told him to take it off. This lasted the entire day. When my wife picked him up from school he collapsed in her arms and cried uncontrollably. He was devastated at how other kids turned on him, even his friends. He asked them to stop but that just made it worse. Only one kid stood up for him. Today he learned how shitty and harmful is toxic masculinity. My rage meter is spiking right now so excuse me if this is a little raw but there are some things I want to say BS gender norms[154]

This incident confirms what we already know which is that gender norms, the ideology behind the gender binary and consequently behind toxic masculinity, are present in the minds of boys from a very early age and certainly before the age of five. Don't assume that this toxicity only kicks in when your son gets to high school. It will be too late by then – chances are he's already well into the cave.

---

[154] https://www.scarymommy.com/dad-thread-toxic-masculinity

You and your partner need to appreciate just how important being tactile is for your child. You kiss him, hug him, comfort him, tell him you love him and praise him as well as chastise him. Be consistent; don't allow your stresses and emotions to dictate your responses to your child. Avoid physical punishment at all costs. If you want a positive punishment for your child, do what an increasing number of schools are now doing around the world; make him sit in a corner and meditate for 10-30 minutes. Schools are increasingly replacing detention with imposed periods of mindfulness, and it works.[155] And you continue the kisses, the hugs, the love strokes all through his life. I still kiss my sons on the lips and they are all grown men. And they kiss me back.

Respect for others is vital. You have to teach it; don't assume he will learn it from school and remember he is definitely unlikely to learn it from his peers. Assume his male peers all have toxic masculinity and proceed accordingly, respect for females being your foremost concern at all times. Explain what is meant by respect, by friendship, by love, and by being a true friend to someone.

Issues around gender awareness need to be introduced before your son goes into the education system. Teach him that some males like males, some females like females, and some children have yet to sort out what they like. Avoid feeding him the stereotypical nuclear family. Also make sure he is aware that some of his friends will have two mummies, some may have two daddies and that this is not unusual. Whatever approach you take, introduce him to diversity. And that must include racial, ethnic and religious diversity. The best schools are now teaching what it means to be LGBT+ and this should start in primary school. But again, don't rely on the school. This is a job for parents. In Scotland, all newly built primary schools now have gender neutral toilets. This will become the norm in progressive countries.[156] I have been involved in helping a leading international school in Hong Kong open the first gender neutral school loo in that city. If it is happening in HK, then it will be happening in many locations. Be prepared for that and prepare your son for what it means.

Make sure he reads books. Real ones with covers and pages. Selecting the right sort of books for him to read is part of this process. A growing number of writers are recognising how toxic masculinity gets reproduced and validated in fiction. Avoid all the superman heroes, or at least make sure you introduce female superheroes also. Writers of children's fiction such as Ben Brooks, Brendan Kiely, J K Rowling, Ed Vere and Robert Muchamore are all producing works which challenge toxic masculinity and fit comfortably with the progressive masculinity narrative. Classic children's books in the progressive genre include

---

[155] https://edition.cnn.com/2016/11/04/health/meditation-in-schools-baltimore/index. html and https://www.theguardian.com/teacher-network/teacher-blog/2013/jun/10/ meditation-mindfulness-schools-stress-calming-classrooms

[156] https://www.breitbart.com/europe/2018/08/06/scotland-children-choose-gender

Peter Pan, the Famous Five, Just William, Where the Wild Things Are, and Harry Potter.[157]

All children are at risk of being bullied and of bullying. I experienced both, especially between the ages of 11 and 14. Nowadays, well managed schools are onto bullying pretty fast, but still it will occur, not only on the school premises but off them. Bullying of LGBT+ children is especially common, but also racist bullying is a big problem. There were over 4,500 school exclusions for racist bullying in the UK during the 2016-17 academic year.[158] This was an increase of nearly 500 on the previous year. Toxic masculinity circulates on the media and gets picked up by children quickly, especially with 24/7 social media. Parents need to prepare for this and the best way is to ensure your child understands what constitutes bullying, that you have a zero-tolerance policy towards it, and that you will support your child if they are bullied. And you do that by going to the school and speaking to the Head and appropriate teachers. Larger schools will employ school counsellors and they can be a most important and valuable resource here.

Children should be exposed to a range of activities which trigger emotional responses, are physically developing, creative and intellectually challenging. I don't see why any of these activities should include using a gun – so no going into the woods with dad, hunting wild beasts. As a child of the 1950s, I was raised on WW2 imagery and using a plastic gun was elementary to my childhood experience. For whatever reason, I never took it further. I was lucky. Far better if your child learns to play the guitar, write a diary, bake a cake, ride a bike and go exploring for insects in the park.

You may consider yourself a liberal parent and that might include you deciding to leave your son to choose his own leisure activities. Don't. No child is totally independent minded. They are merely selecting from the available options. As an adult, you have a better understanding of those options. For example, if he wants to take up boxing at the local gym and you are okay with this, then fine. But make sure he spends more time developing his emotional intelligence rather than his ability to punch someone. His EQ level and the social skills arising from it will be a much better determinant of his future well-being than his sporting prowess.

We all should have aspirations. I am 70 and I still have aspirations. Your son most definitely needs them. Just what those aspirations might be is up to him, but you can and should, guide him. Your first aspiration for your son, in terms of education, should be university. I am not advocating you start talking to him

[157] https://goodmenproject.com/featured-content/childrens-books-that-encourage-non-toxic-masculinity-phtz

[158] https://www.theguardian.com/education/2018/nov/30/record-number-of-uk-children-excluded-for-racist-bullying

about Oxbridge when he's in kindergarten, but he definitely needs to be seeing his educational journey as continuing long after he's 18. This becomes part of the family narrative: university as a given, not an exception. The reasons why your son should go to university are many, but in terms of toxic masculinity university is second only to feminism in terms of being an inoculation against it. Once your son is at university he will be exposed to diverse communities, diverse nationalities, diverse languages and definitely diverse gender and sexual identities. He can only experience it by being in it. Nothing else can prepare him so thoroughly for the 21st century. You can start by taking your son around a local university – a good idea anyway if it has parkland attached to it. Let him feel comfortable in the environment. And when he is at High School, make sure you take him to different university open days, see the students and see inside the lecture theatres, so he might appreciate how mature an environment it is – a world away from school and one he can reasonably aspire to.

Marriages and partnerships break up, more so today than ever in the past. This leaves a lot of children bereft of mum and dad, at least as a physically together family. I know: I was one of those dads. But just because mum and dad are no longer living together doesn't mean your son is destined for toxic masculinity. The father's role is especially important here because we know that toxic masculinity is fed by absent fathers more than by absent mothers. The father must continue regular contact with his child and the mother must allow that and help enable it to happen. Assuming the father-child relationship is not toxic, then most definitely it should not be impinged upon by anyone or any authority. But if the father makes the physical effort – whatever is agreed between him and his ex-partner, in terms of access rights – then that is a commitment above all else and he must stick with it. This is not about the couple's relationship, it is about the father-son relationship. Get this wrong and you'll pay the price. Again, this is something I have learned from personal experience.

The internet is both a blessing and a curse. And if you allow it to dominate your son's life, it will be much more of the latter than the former. Parents must introduce and maintain controls over internet access. Once your son is freely accessing the internet then he is freely accessing everything on the internet, especially if he has his own device. He'll be quickly into VPNs (Virtual Private Networks) and any similar mechanism designed to give him access to porn, especially. If his mates are accessing it, so will he be. This is an important area and one which needs to be agreed by both parents. You decide your rules, but once decided, stick with them. And if necessary, seek assistance from the school. It, too, should have guidelines in place; recommendations for how long a child is on the internet and what time of day such access is allowed.

Sex education is happening to sons every day of the week via the internet. That is unavoidable to some extent, but to avoid toxic masculinity combining with a healthy sexuality to produce a toxic sexuality, you must educate your son in sex and sexuality, and do so in the context of respect for women and LGBT+ people. Approach this from a position of being open-minded and open-hearted. Don't shy away from this responsibility because if you do, then it puts your son at risk, plus any women or girls he gets into a relationship with.

When he is a baby he needs you 100% of the time and you need to be there for him 100% of the time. When he is 22 he still needs you 100% of the time but not with him physically. He is an adult, a man and – you hope – independent. This journey that your son has undertaken is aligned with the journey that you as a parent have undertaken with him. You two shared the journey, shared many of the experiences, the hopes, fears, disappointments and the joys. But as you did so something was happening, or should have been. You should have been growing up: both of you. For your son you hope it means him growing into a man comfortable in his own skin, secure in his progressive masculinity, openly embracing his sexuality, and respectful of others as well as of himself. For you it means growing out of being a parent and into a parentpal. I learned, quite by circumstance, that if you have not achieved a friendship with your son by the time he is 17 then the likelihood is you never will. You have to slowly but resolutely let go of the reins of parenting, or at least loosen them. You seek to replace discipline and control with guidelines and non-judgemental advice. Do this and you'll have a son who is also a friend for life. Don't do it and you'll still have a son, only you won't know who he is. And he won't care to tell you.

My final point is the most important and it relates to the trait I identified above: empathy. Empathy gets learned. Some people find it harder to learn than others, but that little baby who looks at you with his big round eyes and open face is not empathetic by nature. He is an open vessel which you, and society, can fill with the most toxic, brutalising, emotionally crucifying behaviour – if you so choose. To be a parent takes more than love; it takes physical effort and time, both of which are a whole lot more important than money. Your child is going to experience fear, anger, frustration, aggression, anxiety, insecurity, love, friendship, trauma, loss, blissfulness, contentment, irritation, uncertainty … indeed every emotion that you yourself have ever felt. The difference is that your son will experience this while under pressure to conform to toxic masculinity, pressure to strive forward educationally and pressure to be a 'man' – this is when the cave entrance beckons. It happens when his fears and anxieties coalesce around his very natural desire to be accepted into the world as an individual, but a world that may look and sound threatening and alien to him. To retreat into the cave is almost inevitable – almost, not fully. And you can stop it by empathising with him and you do that by recognising his emotions. All parents need to have high levels of empathy. Most parents do acquire empathy towards their child even from the moment they realise one is on the way. It is an immensely powerful emotion. But you also have to develop it in your child. Encourage them to pick up on feelings, facial expressions, body language, verbal language and emotive expressions in others. And get your son or daughter to reflect on why that might be. Especially, encourage them to reflect on their own emotions but in a calm and reasoned way. You may not always be able to provide an answer to their problems or questions, but for sons, learning empathy is far more important and valuable to them than learning sport, passing an exam or being able to use a smartphone. Empathy makes human beings human. And it makes men better men.[159]

---

[159] For details of a UK charity working with young people to prevent domestic abuse and sexual violence, go to https://tender.org.uk

Chapter Eleven

Whither Toxic Masculinity?

Try and imagine a world where any 'Great Men of History' list does not include empire builders, colonialists, conquerors, warriors, soldiers, dictators, autocrats, racists, homophobes or misogynistic bullies. What are we left with? Hopefully we would be left with a list of men who have made a positive difference to humankind, men who have bequeathed us wisdom, beauty, well-being, enlightenment and knowledge.

I am not going to draw up such a list, but one day my grandchildren and their grandchildren may well do so. If so, I hope it has no Napoleons, Caesars or Genghis Khans and instead a lot of Martin Luther Kings, Leonard di Vincis and Buddhas.

More importantly, I hope my offspring and yours are not living in a world which needs or indeed admires men who are good at standing on podiums and shouting populist slogans and rhetoric to the masses, and then encouraging beguiled men to march off to war. Or, just as worrying, feeding fake news via social media to the uncritical masses and thereby undermining precious and fragile democratic processes.

If our offspring are living in such a world then this book, and indeed all books which might conceivably be considered progressive, will have failed in their purpose; for humankind will still be living in the dark ages, even if it is surrounded by every conceivable technology.

Still in the Dark Ages

And right now, humankind is very much in the dark ages. We may have stopped the wholesale slaughter of 'witches' (though not yet in Papua New Guinea); be sending millions of women to university; have landed robots on Mars; be able to wirelessly communicate with others in milliseconds; and passed the Age of Enlightenment by several hundred years; but in terms of men and their masculinity we've barely progressed out of the trees.

If you doubt that, just look around you. Every day you will face countless examples of humanity's continuing addiction to toxic masculinity. When you read of yet another murder, yet another terrorist outrage, yet another rape, yet another venal, bare-faced, lying politician, yet another mass shooting, you are encountering toxic masculinity. You can see it in the intractable conflicts of the Middle East, the post-colonial horrors of Africa, the global drug trade, global sex trafficking, the stoning to death of an 'adulterous woman' in Afghanistan, the whipping of LGBT people in Indonesia, and in a global criminal underclass. But more even than this, the codes and values that sustain toxic masculinity are present in our competitively ruthless and punishingly unequal global capitalist system, in the political conditions that force millions into poverty and homelessness, in the avid weaponisation of society and in the degradation of the environment and extinction of species.

Right now, we are all living and breathing toxic masculinity. We may have named it, but we certainly haven't erased it. While life in the 21st century is a whole lot better for the vast majority of people than it was for their ancestors, we have not yet progressed to a level whereby we can honestly and truthfully claim to be 'civilised'. I certainly recognise progress, but whatever peace and civilisation we have is wafer thin. If you or your loved ones are brutalised, assaulted, violated or are refugees from terror or brutal discrimination, then civilisation has broken down not just for you, but for all of us. If any woman, anywhere in the world, cannot go out at night on her own without fear of male attack, then we are not civilised. If the only peaceful existence is to be had in privileged gated communities and society needs to incarcerate millions of males to keep it that way, then civilisation still has a long way to go.

Do we blame men for the state of the world? Well, males have been the gender that exercised the most control over humanity's direction since we walked out of Africa, so maybe we should. Certainly they have failed miserably in many areas, not least the eradication of violence. That, for me, is as good justification as is needed to ensure we have a future where women hold the balance of power, not men. Women can bring qualities which most men, right now, do not possess. But not just women. We also need men with progressive masculinity to step up and lead humanity. Whatever their sex and gender, humanity needs leaders who are not toxic. Because if we replace male toxic leaders with women toxic leaders then not much changes.

It seems events in the early 21st century force humanity to look deep into itself. And what humanity sees is not very comforting. The number of disorientating 'black swan' moments appears to be multiplying, not diminishing. We can certainly see them in Brexit, Trump, Syria, Putin, religious fundamentalism, a resurgent nationalist discourse and the global refugee crisis, looming environmental catastrophe, but also in global mental health problems, global trade stand-offs, and the insidious undermining of democratic values by those with a toxic agenda, notably via social media. This has triggered a loss of confidence and a loss of hope in many. This is desperately sad, especially for the young people most affected by this. As a father of five and an educationalist, that matters to me a lot. No doubt it does to you too.

But perhaps looking deep into ourselves is something we are long overdue. When the myths finally get removed we are left with reality, and reality is what we must ultimately face. It may not be pleasant to expose men and toxic masculinity, but it is essential we do so. This is the only way out of the cave.

Much as we might want change, we should recognise it won't come from others. It will only come from ourselves. We have to expect more of ourselves, not of others. Any change will come from the individual. It won't come from how we vote, how often we pray, how much we spend, or from wielding a weapon. It can only come from how we relate to others, and that requires empathy and understanding. If we change for the better, then the world changes for the better. That is all it takes.

As I see it, eradicating toxic masculinity is central to any positive transformation of society. Indeed, it always has been, only now we are starting to recognise it. This moment of awareness is critical to the future and we need to keep it going, allow it to grow and take root in society especially in our children. Develop the conversation, feed the narrative, not just in the West or with the educated middle classes, but worldwide. This growing awareness mirrors a growing maturity in society and maturity is going to be needed if society is to come out of the gender dark ages. That the critical gaze has finally shifted to men and their masculinities gives me hope. Because it shows there is a new conversation taking place globally. And for the first time in history, men are the focus; not the mythical, heroic male project of yesteryears, but instead a reflective and critical look at how men behave and how they can be helped to become better men. Men always needed to be the focus. Feminism has always been more about changing men than changing women. At least now, more men are listening and acting.

At the Crossroads

So where does this leave us? I am not sure. What I do know is that humanity is at a crossroads and the next few decades will decide it. But it is unclear which direction humanity will go in. There are conflicting and contradictory indicators and how one interprets these trends depends on where one is positioned in our globalised world. In this book I have claimed that there is a very clear trend towards more power for women and that is evidenced by the rising voices of women, the growth of a female educated middle class, the increase in women in leadership and managerial positions across the spectrum, and the whole global resurgence of feminism. I am in no doubt about this trend, not least because I've had 70 years of experiencing it and observing it, the last 30 years very intensely. In tandem with this rise in women's power is a decline in traditional femininity and the rise of the 'super solo society'. These trends are definitely related and they all connect to men's continued adherence to toxic masculinity.

As far as the future is concerned, we can do no more than speculate. But that is fine because speculation has value. We may not know the future, but we can surely sketch out the options, the possibilities. And the possibilities as I see them, are as follows:

Scenario 1: Patriarchal backlash

Scenario 2: Female future aligned with toxic masculinity

Scenario 3: The collapse of masculinity: a sort of androgyny

Scenario 4: Feminist future aligned with progressive masculinity

What follows is simply my interpretation as to the possible future scenarios arising from the revolutionary shifts in gender dynamics, gender power and gender awareness. This revolution certainly has momentum currently, though it has been gathering pace in terms of rising social awareness at least since the late 1800s. However, in considering future scenarios, I am only marginally concerned with what I term peripheral variables; economics, social class, technology, globalisation, war, environmental disaster, religion, terrorism, media, health, education, migration, social unrest, artificial intelligence, nationalism, and racism. Firstly, I claim no expertise in most of these fields of study and human activity. Secondly, all these variables are underpinned by gender; they each, in direct and indirect ways, relate to gender identity, for the reason that human identity is gendered. Thirdly, each of these fields has been historically dominated by man and masculinism, and although that continues to be the case, women are no longer invisible within them. To put it another way, the historical gender binary is the template which defines these variables. Not one of them exists outside the historical gender order. Therefore it is reasonable to expect that each will be influenced by changes to that historical gender order. The variables primarily stem from how men and women have historically seen themselves as individuals and how they relate to each other as gendered and sexual subjects. If or when that self-awareness shifts and impacts on everyday practice, so then does everything around it shift also. We are already seeing that process at work in relation to the emergence of a 'super solo society'. That phenomenon acts like a social tsunami, impacting on housing, economics, birth-rates, globalisation, education, migration, the environment, health and so on.

In my seven decades I have never had the sense that humanity is at such a profound crossroads as I do today. To be sure, the Cuban missile crisis, the Vietnam War, the Cold War, the Maoist Revolution, the Arab-Israeli wars and the break-up of the imperialist empires were each a critical and decisive event of the second half of the 20th century. But they did not trigger the same level of existential anxiety as we see around us today. They certainly resulted in death and despair for millions of people, but there was always the sense that they were merely continuations of history; even in their brutal effects they simply confirmed nothing had changed. If there was an 'end of history' during the late 20th century, it was not the consequence of women or men changing. In that respect, horrific events as humanity had always experienced them simply continued to occur.

What we are experiencing and feeling today is much more complex. Yes, we are a lot less likely to die from war and pestilence than our ancestors, but we have lost innocence along the way. If, as I suspect, global society is maturing then it is also rupturing. Some describe this as 'culture wars', others refer it to 'identity politics'. However we define it, we can sense this is different to our ancestors' obsession with the politics of left and right. And that can be threatening and dangerous because people may be persuaded to change their viewpoint over an issue of politics, but they will be much less willing to change their viewpoint over an issue of identity, and even less so over gender and sexual identities.

Therefore, the question remains as to what happens next. Are we emerging out of the gender dark ages? Is the currently highly tentative 'civilising process' likely to continue with positive consequences for every human being? Is the rise of women to be pushed back or pushed forward? Or are we heading for androgynous future?

Scenario 1: Patriarchal Backlash

The notion of a male backlash is not new and indeed Susan Faludi was one of the first feminist writers to examine this scenario in her two books *Backlash* (1992) and *Stiffed* (1999).[160]

> *Why don't contemporary men rise up in protest at their betrayal? If they have experienced so many of the same injuries as women, the same humiliations, why don't they challenge the culture as women did? Why can't men seem to act?... Men aren't simply refusing to "give up the reins of power", as some feminist have argued. The reins have already slipped from most of their hands, anyway.*[161]

Of course, Faludi's thesis is more about the plight of US working-class men, and it can be argued their condition is the result of economic factors, notably the

[160] Faludi, S. (1991) *Backlash.* London: Vintage; Faludi S. (1999) *Stiffed.* London: Chatto & Windus.

[161] Faludi, S. (1999) *Stiffed.* (p. 603)

emergence of globalisation, not the rise of women or indeed feminism. While this class of men lacked material wealth, they did retain a sense of themselves which drew heavily on toxic masculine values and assumptions, and like working class men everywhere, they did resist women's emancipation both at work and in their own families. In that regard they are not unusual, because men of whatever class have always fought against the tide of gender change, certainly any change that might result in a loss of male power: men battled the suffragettes; they made sure women returned to the kitchen after contributing to both world wars; and at no point during the last century did a mass of men unilaterally take the lead in empowering and liberating women from political, economic, gender, sexual, social or material discrimination. They could have done. After all, they were the ones holding the reins of power. But they either actively resisted or they passively resisted. Even today, over two years after MeToo, there are relatively few men prepared to stand up and join women in this fight. Too many prefer to be bystanders, passive in their resistance; resisting by distancing; resisting by complaining about 'political correctness having gone too far'; resisting by appearing to be supporters but secretly hoping the MeToo phenomenon disappears as fast as it arrived.

In which case, a future patriarchal backlash scenario can reasonably be described as men simply continuing to behave as they have always done; that is, uniting in resistance when confronted with the wrath and frustration of women who say 'enough' and who demand material change. From that premise, this scenario is perhaps the most likely. We can already see the signs in the incel 'movement', in a deepening and more explicit male fundamentalism and in the hatred which misogynists openly spit out at women on the internet. We can see the signs in the rising nationalistic discourse around the world and made explicit in Brexit, Trump, Putin and a host of third-tier nationalist politicians shouting their rhetoric from Brazil to Hungary.

Technology is an important variable here. Far from being a device of human liberation, it is proving to be a device enabling humans to continue toxifying each other. Speed, access, openness and anonymity all play their part, which is an early warning that advanced technology does not automatically lead to enlightenment. It is equally if not more likely to simply expose, if not intensify, the biases, hatreds, prejudices, intolerances and fears already festering in human minds. In which case, any hope that AI will be somehow gender neutral, non-racist, pro-LGBT+ and generally benign is likely to prove misguided. AI will be designed by humans and will therefore be a mirror of those human's own deeply held prejudices and subjectivities.

In which case, we should ask ourselves this: has the patriarchal backlash already started or has it never gone away? Both. It never went away and it could be just getting started. It is definitely now re-forming itself in tandem with the available outlets, the primary outlets for this backlash being politics and technology, both of which can be – and are being – used against women.

A prime example of this is China. China is a remarkable country and I admire its people enormously. But it is neither women friendly, feminist friendly, nor LGBT+ friendly. Being a declared feminist in China is a decidedly risky proposition. While I recognise the Chinese government's over-riding concern is to maintain internal stability and ensure the 1 billion of its population who still remain locked in poverty continue to be relatively passive, the fact is that freedom of expression will be the price to pay. There are already signs of a patriarchal backlash occurring in China, not least with the drive to control education; monitor the population 24/7 via the internet, AI and the new social credit system; encourage the 'training of boys to be men'; and restrict any feminist or pro LGBT+ discourse, e.g. shutting down feminist webchat groups, feminist centres, and anti-sexual violence centres.[162]

But China is not alone. Putin's Russia is equally guilty of encouraging a backlash against liberal values, feminism, LGBT+ rights and any serious change in the condition of women. Russia's retardedly masculinist form of government is never going lead the world to a feminist era. An even more disturbing example is India, generally recognised to be one of the worst countries in the world to be born female; with rape, abuse and misogyny all firmly embedded in the cultural, economic and political landscape of that country. If we add in most of Africa, South America, Central America, parts of South East Asia, the Middle East and Eastern Asia, then we are not left with too many places where it is good to be born female, even today. And there isn't one country where a woman can live her life absolutely 100% sure of never being subjected to male violence.

Whatever the country, it now exists in a global capitalist economy and while there is evidence to show this system has taken hundreds of millions out of women out of poverty, capitalism remains largely dominated by male leaders and a masculinist work culture, with women the first to feel the consequences of any economic slowdown. Many commenters are already suggesting women will suffer disproportionately more than men once AI starts taking jobs. Certainly, with AI looming, it doesn't look hopeful that women will be closing the global gender pay gap any time before 2220, at least according to recent research by the World Economic Forum.[163]

[162] https://www.scmp.com/news/china/society/article/2176973/china-gender-and-sexuality-centre-shuts-down-censorship-chill

[163] https://www.iwecfoundation.org/news/the-global-gender-gap-report-2018-from-world-economic-forum

And then there is the problem of religion. Every main religion, in its organisation and dominant cultural expression, encourages patriarchal discourses and discourages feminist ones. This makes organised religion the enemy of feminists and of progressive men everywhere. This is not a slur on the underpinning spiritual values of any religion; it is simply a condemnation of the toxic men who have historically defined, interpreted and led such religions and who still largely prevail within them.

A patriarchal backlash is then the easiest option for men, not least because it will be aided by prevailing masculinist cultures and systems. Men can merely return to form, behave in a way they always have when faced with anything which might reduce their power over women, plus it means they don't have to go through any unpleasant critical self-reflection.

But there may be a further dimension to this backlash, which is that it might be expressed as a resurgence of misogynistic feelings. In this scenario one can see that MeToo happened so fast and led to such a torrent of global criticism against toxic masculinity that men were caught off guard. They really did experience this as an emotional punch in the gut. And once they regain their breath, then they will lash out like never before. We could already be at the tipping point when reasonable men stop listening to the criticism, stop looking inward, stop recognising that women have a point, stop questioning their masculinity, and instead seek to reassert it and themselves. This backlash will definitely be aided by some 'neutral scientific experts', claiming that there is no patriarchy, that men are the victims and that male and female brain constitution really does mean they come from different planets.

The incels and male fundamentalists are examples of how far such a reassertion might go, driven as it is by fear, defensiveness, rage and hatred towards women and Others. In other words, men stop being defensive and instead feel rage at women, 'political correctness' and liberal values generally, and that rage gets channelled into nationalism, fascism, authoritarianism, religious extremism, criminality, violence and an attempt to close down the feminist discourse completely. This is definitely the worse-case scenario but one which many men around the world today would like to see come to fruition.

Whatever the level of the backlash it will inevitably be framed around an anti-feminist rhetoric. Recognising that the 'feminist' label is used by toxic men pejoratively and applied to any woman with an independent mind and voice, then in reality, the backlash will be against all women. And if it is against all women, then it is against all LGBT+ people and against all progressive straight men. Which is why all women should be feminists and wherever possible strive for positions of power and authority, with every progressive man in active support of them.

Scenario 2: Female Future Aligned with Toxic Masculinity

One of the topics I have so far avoided is that of 'toxic femininity', largely because this book is not concerned with femininity but also because I don't intend to undertake excursions into those areas peripheral to toxic masculinity. However, this does not mean that toxic femininity does not exist, nor am I suggesting that all women are angels with blessed natures. Clearly that is not the case. Women can be homophobic, racist, fascist and generally toxic just like men can be. The notion that 'power tends to corrupt and absolute power corrupts absolutely' applies to humans of whatever gender and sexuality. At the same time, while society should always have a critical eye on the powers that be, right now humanity's problems are overwhelmingly with male power, not female power. Female power is on the rise but it remains far from being so ubiquitous as to present a problem in its own right.

However, that could well change.

At this point we need to briefly revisit the concept of 'identity', discussed in Chapter 2. The key point is that identity is a process, not an outcome, and it is a process always contingent on the social environment within which it is practised. Social environments change and if nothing else can be predicted about the human condition, we can certainly be sure our social environments will not remain static. And by changing, so will people. Children born today will be a whole lot different to children born even twenty years ago, and certainly different from those born in my era. This is the way human nature is; it adapts, alters, shifts and reacts. And it is reacting now, albeit in ways which won't become apparent until some time after the event.

There is nothing innate in men which makes them aggressive, domineering and violent. Nor is there anything innate in women which makes them passive, demure and motherly. There are as many differences between women and between men as there are between women and men. Men can behave like women, and women can behave like men. You don't need me to alert you to this; you will already have witnessed the fluidity of gender identity in your own life.

However, recent research on girls and violence in the US, Australia and the UK, all confirms a worrying trend:

A growing number of teenage girls are engaging in extreme not-so-nice behaviour, including violence'. 'While boys commit more antisocial crimes than girls, the rate of girls being charged with violent crimes has increased twice as fast as boys. In recent years, female offenders are entering the juvenile justice system at a younger age and at a higher rate... Boys and girls are more similar in the rate of aggression in urban schools than in rural schools.[164]

[164] Meichenbaum, D. (2013) *Comparison of Aggression in Boys and Girls: A Case for Gender-Specific Interventions.* Miami, Florida: Melissa Institute; and https://www.fatherly.com/health-science/physical-aggression-boys-girls-fighting

If we imagine that females will always be the 'better angels of human nature' then we are into dangerous territory. Indeed, we are in the same dangerous territory as that which suggests all men have toxic masculinity. Stereotypes are at best misleading and invariably downright damaging. We must not slip into the myths of femininity any more than we must slip into the myths of masculinity. At the same time, any man reading that statement who therefore imagines it 'lets him off the hook' in terms of critically analysing his own masculinity is missing the point completely. Society is not damaged by femininity, but what it can be damaged by is women moving into positions of power and along the way picking up the toxic masculinity virus.

As I described in the opening chapter, toxic masculinity is on the wind; it is discursive. It is not rooted in the biology of human nature, it is not in our genes. The only reason why men gravitate towards it is because it has traditionally served to validate male identity. Which is why women have not gravitated towards it. But that 'comfortable' arrangement can easily change and indeed it may well be doing so.

If females begin to imagine that being a woman requires them to be selfish, aggressive, egotistical, domineering and emotionally inhibited, that true femininity is not sweet but hard, and to be this way they need to copy the behaviours of men, then society has a problem. We may well end up with a future dominated by females but the females who dominate will be scarcely different from the men who dominate today.

This scenario is not that far-fetched. We already have females achieving far higher levels of education than males, and we already have women moving into powerful positions in business, commerce, politics, media and most every other profession. These two trends do look unstoppable at the moment and I certainly hope they are unstoppable. However, recognising the trajectory, it is therefore most important, and indeed in humanity's interest, as well as the interest of women and LGBT+ people, that women in power are feminists, not surrogate sisters of toxic masculinity.

Is this scenario likely? Yes, it is, which is why I have raised it. But how likely I have no idea. It is simply one of the four paths currently facing humanity. It may be the least likely path, or not. What will determine the outcome will be to what extent feminist values prevail in global society and especially how successful we are at teaching such values to the younger generation, both male and female. Right now, toxic masculinity is dominant, though not without resistance. But if that resistance falters and the ideology behind toxic masculinity strengthens and women continue to move into positions of power but do so by adopting masculinist values, then we could end up with toxic masculinity being replaced by a feminine version, the primary difference being it is practised by humans with vaginas, not humans with penises.

163

What might a feminine version of toxic masculinity look like? It would be a way of being a woman that is fundamentally embedded in the current capitalist system, but one which has transformed into a global super solo society; where men and women are failing to connect intimately, living singular lifestyles, increasingly narcissistic, materialistic, selfish, inward-looking, and pursuing individuality not communality. The women would have power through wealth, education and social status, be pursuing relationships primarily for instrumental and functional reasons, not having children, and treating men as disposable assets. I don't see women's future power being heavily invested in physical strength and violence as it is with men, but that scenario could easily change once Artificial Intelligence fully enters society. With AI, the very notion of physical threat will change from being predominantly human in orientation to being robotic. Likewise, protection from physical harm will also be robotic rather than human. In other words, physicality won't be reliant on human muscle power.

The aim of feminism is not now and never has been to create women with traditional masculinity, nor indeed men with traditional femininity. That said, we are now seeing straight men performing femininity and there is little doubt we are also seeing straight women perform masculinity. Inevitably, femininity is changing, it is becoming more confident, more assertive and in some instances more aggressive. It is also becoming more violent, albeit mostly with girls in urban areas. The traditional femininity of the past is going or has gone. Whether or not it ever existed other than in the imagination and in myth is, of course, a relevant question. But whether real or myth, it is increasingly being rejected as an identity option by a new generation of women who are choosing to express their femininity in ways closely aligned with masculinity. How far this will go, and to what extent will emerge a feminine version of toxic masculinity prevailing across society is, for now, still speculation.

Scenario 3: The Collapse of Masculinity: A Sort of Androgyny

I deliberately played with this scenario in my opening to Chapter 5, partly because I can envision this coming into existence, but also because I find it the most intriguing, if somewhat extreme, of the four scenarios. I am not claiming a global 'collapsed masculinity' will emerge anytime soon, but in terms of where we stand at the crossroads, we may already be on this particular path albeit without realising it.

Certainly Japan, South Korea, the major Eastern cities of China and Hong Kong are already heading in this direction, to the extent that many regional politicians and social commentators are shouting in alarm. And from their perspective they are right to do so, because a collapse of masculinity will change everything.

It will seriously diminish the power of what Dwight D Eisenhower famously called the 'military-industrial complex'. It will change the nature of work and correspondingly, the nature of global capitalism. It will fit perfectly well with the rise of AI, the decline of traditional employment patterns, the rise of the sexbot and the need to reduce the world population to manageable, healthy levels. This, in turn, will have a positive impact on the environment to the point that, hopefully, we are no longer at risk of a monumental catastrophe from global warming. It will match the apparently growing desire of men and women to live apart, not together, and it will ensure the super solo society is not toxic but progressive or at least sustainable and harmonious. And society should be a lot more harmonious, because there will be much less male violence; the incel will have all but disappeared along with male fundamentalism, leaving us able to reduce prison populations, spend more on health and education, and not fearing to go out at night in case we get attacked by some madman. Global criminality will be on the wane. Why? Because a short, brutal life of macho-criminality will become as unattractive for these men as signing up for the army and going to war against strangers. It also fits with the growing secularisation of society, with humans increasingly in pursuit of their individual spiritual path outside of organised religion – no longer 'cultural dopes' of radical, simplistic narratives and ideologies. Finally, the collapse of masculinity enables women to move into positions of power and influence more readily, not least because men will be much less interested in sacrificing their lives to any career, employer or rigid work system: they will have no masculinity in need of validation through work, power, dominance, wealth and status. They will have no logical reason to resist women's empowerment, nor desire to.

All this will be aided by, and correspond with, the ongoing massification of higher education; the rise of the concept of 'global citizen'; improvements in the mental health of both sexes; a less stridently competitive and unequal society; an appreciation that emotional intelligence is more valuable than material capital; and the general enlightenment which hopefully should envelop society once toxic masculinity disappears.

The negative is that women and men, because they will be behaving almost identically, will cease to be attracted to each other. Of course, as I discuss in chapter 7, AI is already moving to fill that gap for millions (mostly men), but it will still leave society bereft of physical intimacy between the sexes. Men and women may get sexual release from robots or choose to be celibate; they may even experience a form of love with their interactive 'Lovot',[165] but it will be a sad day if humanity is reduced to this. A further negative is one which is already with us: the decline of parenting. Millions around the world today will never

[165] https://www.bangkokpost.com/tech/1596734/lovot-aims-to-spread-a-little-love

experience the joys of being a parent, nor will they learn from this experience. Recent research by the London School of Economics reveals that 'fathers are less likely to hold traditional views about gender if they raise a girl.'[166] That increasing numbers of men are going to be deprived of this learning curve can be of no comfort to anyone concerned with the future of gender relationships.

This growing apart of men and women has definitely been a trend for some decades now and the collapse of masculinity is, in many ways, about men confirming this by saying 'I am okay no longer trying to dominate anyone and behaving like an alpha male'. This can be interpreted as 'I no longer see women as different and unknowable, I want to be like them.'

This, then, leads us to a sort of androgynous future, a world where identity is not defined by genitalia but more through agency.

Currently, sex identity provides the most compelling and powerful identity template; that template then emerges as gender identity, largely through osmosis. But what if society can disregard the original sex template? If that happens then gender disappears. Already we have families attempting this, notably by actively ensuring their child grows up surrounded by 'gender neutral' imagery and language, with increasing numbers of families withholding the sex of their child until after the child learns some independence. But that can only be maintained for as long as the parent controls the child's environment. Once the child is out in society then sex and gender influences kick in. There seems no way of avoiding the binary.

But the binary would already have ceased to exist in the event of a global collapse in masculinity. The emergence of both the feminoid male and a more masculine femininity suggest this. In which case, physical sex identification will no longer automatically be the template upon which gender and all ensuing identities are generated. Instead, men and women will converge in their identities rather than exist in some rigid division of 'macho men' and 'demure women'.

That sections of global society are already on this path is unquestionable, but what we don't yet know is whether this is a temporary diversion from the ongoing saga of humanity's addiction to toxic masculinity, or the beginning of a totally new story.

Scenario 4: Feminist Future Aligned With Progressive Masculinity

If you've read this far then you'll probably realise this would be my preferred scenario. However, it does come at a price and that price will be mostly paid by men. If men are prepared to pay that price, which is effectively an end to their historic gender power and a complete erasure of toxic masculine behaviour,

[166] http://www.lse.ac.uk/News/Latest-news-from-LSE/2018/12-December-2018/%EF%BB%BFFathers-less-likely-to-hold-sexist-attitudes-if-they-have-a-girl

then there is no doubt humanity can achieve a scenario where men and women live more harmoniously, supportively, empathetically, productively and safely; women and children no longer subject to harassment, violence and abuse, men no longer violent towards each other. Women and men no longer growing apart and finding solace in robotic sex, singledom and a 'super solo society', but rather in intimate relationships. Humans no longer concerned with an individual's gender, sexuality, race or ethnicity but embracing each other as equals and with mutual respect.

In this scenario we will have become civilised, not just a relatively privileged, protected few but all of us.

Right now, some men are definitely moving in this direction, others are unsure and confused and a lot are either passively resisting or actively resisting.

The standpoint position must be that we cannot continue to accept toxic masculinity as the 'normal' or acceptable way of being a man. I recognise this will create problems for many men and it is already doing so. During the week I wrote this chapter a Welsh father of two apparently committed suicide after being accused of inappropriate behaviour at a staff Christmas party by two female colleagues.[167] Since 2017, the cultural landscape has dramatically shifted and most men are still working out the new rules. This fast-emerging cultural paradigm will bring new legislation, new expectations, new languages, new definitions and certainly intense pressure on men to change their mindset and their practices. This won't just be in a few countries' it will eventually become global. And it will happen despite the active resistance of many powerful men.

I also recognise that wholesale change across all of humanity is asking a lot of humanity. With 7.5 billion of us already here, the idea that we can all move in tandem in a particular direction is unfeasible and unrealistic. Or is it? At least now we have global communications and an instant information society. This results in social and cultural trends developing very fast. If humanity continues to look deep into itself and question its past then it may well make the effort to create a better future. MeToo is an excellent example of how traditional toxic behaviours can quickly get challenged and changed.

But to get to this scenario we are going to need more than MeToo. We are going to have to challenge and then detoxify a masculinist work culture and economic system that has been designed to encourage, not discourage, toxic masculine behaviour. We will need an education system less concerned with intellectual achievement and much more focused on EQ; empathy, respect, understanding, reflexivity and tolerance for all. We will have to strengthen the liberal democratic processes and resist the temptation to succumb to toxic

---

[167] https://www.telegraph.co.uk/news/2018/12/27/father-two-found-dead-allegations-made-following-lawyers-christmas

masculinist populist alt-right agendas. And we need to be better parents, avoiding spreading the toxic masculine virus down through the generations.

Basically, whether or not you believe this scenario is achievable depends on your faith in humanity. Are we destined to appear civilised only on the surface, but in our minds and behaviours remain addicted to a gender performance which cripples humanity? Or can we be better than that?

Can men be better than they have been?

That question now hangs in the air. How it gets answered will determine our future.

NOTES

About the Author

Dr Stephen M Whitehead has previously authored and edited 12 books including *Men and Masculinities* (Polity), *Gender and Identity* (Oxford University Press), *The Masculinities Reader* (Polity), *Men and Masculinities* (Routledge), *Managing Professional Identities* (Routledge), *The Many Faces of Men* (Arrow), *The Relationship Manifesto* (Andrews UK), *My Dark Side* (Andrews UK), *International Schooling: The Teacher's Guide* (Pedagogue). He is currently writing *Total Inclusivity: what it means for your organisation and for you* (forthcoming) and *Creating the Totally Inclusive School* (Routledge, forthcoming). Stephen's books have been translated into 17 languages. He has lectured on men and masculinities and changing gender identities at leading global universities and international schools. He now lives in Chiang Mai, Thailand. For more information about Stephen and his works, check out these websites:

www.stephenwhitehead.org
www.stephen-whitehead.com
www.totalinclusivity.com
www.whiteheadlee.com

Lightning Source UK Ltd.
Milton Keynes UK
UKHW010705210622
404740UK00001B/165

9 781789 825251